English Translation: Marion Shapiro

Living Architecture:

ANCIENT MEXICAN

TEXT AND PHOTOGRAPHS BY **HENRI STIERLIN**

Preface by VLADIMIR KASPE

Macdonald · London

Editor of Series   Henri Stierlin
Plans   Jean Duret FAS SIA

SBN   356 00763 4
Printed in Switzerland
Photo-composition   Filmsatz AG, Berne
Printing Text and Plans   Buri Druck, Berne
Heliogravure plates   Heliographia S.A., Lausanne
Offset reproductions   Aberegg-Steiner & Cie S.A., Berne
Binding   Max Grollimund, Basle

© Office du Livre   Published by
Fribourg 1968   Macdonald & Co. (Publishers) Ltd.,
49 Poland Street, London W. 1.

Contents

The Legacy of the pre-Columbian past in modern Mexican architecture

What has the contemporary Mexican architect inherited from the pre-Columbian past? And does it still have any influence? Are there living relationships between a seemingly complete past and a continually changing present?

These questions cannot be given straightforward or facile answers. Every architect is an isolated case – according to his origins, his era, his teaching, the extent of his culture, and a thousand other chance happenings during his lifetime. The preface that follows is therefore based partly on what I have observed among my colleagues, but primarily on my twenty-five years' experience of professional practice in Mexico.

In Europe, 16th-century architecture shares nothing with present-day concepts, but it is none the less the ancestor of contemporary architecture. In Mexico, however, the era that preceded the Conquest is further removed from us by far.

There was a complete break in religion, thought and in social and technical progress as seen from a western viewpoint. Contact with 'pre-western' architecture cannot therefore be direct. However, some vivid aspects of the past architecture still survive and, despite everything, are close to contemporary Mexican architecture, sometimes closer even than the European past.

What is responsible for the vitality and permanence of its forms?

Nature

The ties binding us to various concepts of pre-Columbian architecture derive primarily from nature, which is itself permanent. It has influenced and continues to influence the face of Mexican architecture. Nature has a bearing on our knowledge of the architecture of the past; and through nature, past creations live and still have a message for us.

Characteristic broad landscape in the Mexican high plateaux

The Mexican climate generally follows an unchanging pattern. Extreme cold is unknown; the sun shines for most of the year. Trees, plants, flowers, never really alter.

Owing to differences in altitude the landscape is extremely varied but always impressive. Mountains, snow-covered, green, or bare, endless valleys, unusual species of tropical plants, deserts, beaches, lakes and waterfalls – everything is on a grand scale. Nowadays, planes, helicopters, automobiles and aerial photography have added to our awareness of the magnificence of the Mexican landscape.

Because the air is extraordinarily transparent, our perception of nature is immediate, even at great distances. We can see contours clearly, the bold contrasts between shadow and light, the relief of volumes, the vivid colors. The blue sky seems to stretch into infinity, and the constantly moving clouds add to this impression of unbounded space.

Above all is the sense of grandeur that has encouraged man to form broad and fruitful concepts.

The architecture of the past

The early builders treated space – which is nature's finest gift to man – with remarkable intelligence and sensitivity. They achieved what modern architects and town planners continually advocate: to 'compose' with space.

This they did on a truly grandiose scale: in the connections between the great sanctuaries or terraces preceding the buildings and the neighboring landscape, in the direct relation between these planned spaces and the architecture itself, in the deepest penetration of space through porticoes and entrances, in the treatment of the horizontal or vertical lines of moldings, and in the geometrical or stylized motifs sculpted over the entire surfaces of walls.

In every way, the ancient Mexican architect showed a deep understanding of the possibilities nature offers. First, by the choice and use of stone. Hard or soft, white, grey, golden or mauve, according to regions or needs, the architect knew how to obtain textures and could dress stone so that it not only fulfilled its function but also reflected the Mexican sunlight. Furthermore, he remained so close to nature that it is sometimes difficult to decipher where the original state ends and man's work begins.

Constructional methods – during the periods dealt with in this book – are characterized by the predominance of the rectangle over every other geometric form. Despite numerous details, this results in a remarkable simplicity of forms and volumes. The masses are conceived to be seen from a distance and to contrast with their vast surroundings: we see them distinctly and as a whole. The contours are simple but never harsh; the projections are numerous but never complicated; the ornamentation rich but never excessive.

Sometimes the play of masses is opposed to plain and mountain; sometimes it imitates the latter (the pyramids). Man imposes or adapts. The variety of concepts is infinite. Yet the predecessors of contemporary Mexican architecture all have 'decision' as well as 'control'. Two human qualities that have rarely joined in such a successful synthesis.

The architecture of the present

Let us return to the elements that we mentioned in connection with the past: first, the sense of space.

Space in Mexico, as we have seen, can only be conceived on a grand scale. The early architects were well aware of this and for contemporary Mexican architects it is an indispensable element. Moreover, our programs are often on a very large scale: hospitals, universities, schools, factories, urban complexes. Although we also work with smaller units – houses, furniture, etc. – we tend more and more towards group programs as the only way to solve innumerable urgent problems, and also to attain the unity that characterized pre-Columbian architecture at its height.

There are two principles of composition that the contemporary Mexican architect has readopted from his predecessors, developing them as he adapts them to his programs: first, that of open spaces – in front of, around and within both public and private buildings, treating the spaces as sanctuaries, courtyards, terraces or gardens. Second, the principle of the most direct contact between interior and exterior space.

Aluminium sun-screens on the south-east corner of the central offices of the 'Supermarchés' Company, S.A. of Mexico, by Vladimir Kaspé, 1961

The garden-patio of the central offices of the 'Super-marchés' Company S.A., by Vladimir Kaspé, 1961

The application of these principles is particularly striking in the new Museo de Antropologia, the University City or the Polytechnic Institute at Mexico City, the arrangement of the approaches to the convent at Tepotzotlan, the numerous medical centers throughout the country, etc.

The range of materials used today is evidently greater than those of the pre-Columbian era: marble, brick, concrete, wood, metal, synthetic substances, as well as stone. Yet stone continues to be widely employed, not only for thermic protection but because it is the most effective means of obtaining plastic effects. It forms a kind of intimate 'pact' between sky and earth.

Finally, from a formal viewpoint, the dynamic lines and volumes of pre-Columbian architecture continue to inspire us. For numerous reasons: first, because we are, like our predecessors, trying to affirm and place architecture in the landscape with strength and daring. We also have a taste for dynamic forms, even though it is based on different origins. The sensibility of a man who travels by automobile undergoes a transformation. He has to perceive immediately and completely the effect and significance of the architectural frame through which he moves. The scale of the town, continually developing and his chief 'landscape,' must be always intelligible to him. From this point of view the effects sought after and obtained by pre-Columbian architects serve our new purposes admirably.

There is yet another element common to both past and present Mexican architecture: the past has shown us that the simplest, even elementary, effects are the most effective, and the present, due to the need for economy and the taste for what is concrete, also abhors complication. The sun, the transparent air, and ever-present nature serve to emphasize the most modest concept.

In this preface we have mentioned only 'indirect' ties—undoubtedly numerous—that exist between the builders of a distant but vigorous era, and those who are constantly trying to make contemporary architecture more 'real'. The latter cannot afford to adopt extreme or preconceived attitudes towards the past.

The outstanding contributions of contemporary Mexican architects are indissolubly linked with nature, which has nourished them, with the past that impassions them, and with the present (or future, virtually the same) which they approach with enthusiasm and faith. The successful combination of these different elements is responsible for our architecture which, while in perfect harmony with the ideas of so-called international architecture, still possesses its own individual and remarkably fascinating character.

Mexico, January 1967

1. The Common bases in pre-Columbian cultures

If a historian's interest in architecture is proportionate to what it teaches about man, then pre-Columbian buildings have a special value, since the architecture of ancient Mexico is our primary source of information about the Middle American civilizations. Books, chronicles and hieroglyphics have almost wholly vanished, together with mathematical and astronomical systems, and we are left with only traces of their astonishingly advanced learning. Architecture, however, provides us with highly important facts about them. In addition to buildings and construction techniques, it helps us to understand the religious, social and economic organization of a whole culture. It reveals the structure and extent of different cosieties; it shows the relationships, the areas of influence and contacts between civilizations. Finally, it enables us to understand the hierarchy, the technology and functions of various social groups.

Architecture, moreover, is never isolated: related arts all contribute to make it a major source of information. We know the role played in forms of worship by sculpture and, particularly, statuary, as well as painting and frescoes decorating sanctuaries and palaces. Pre-Columbian architecture is the directing element in a great synthesis of the arts: all forms of esthetic expression are subordinated to it. It is therefore impossible to disassociate architecture as such from its environment. This total aspect of building forces us to study every form of ancient Mexican construction.

Architecture thus represents more than a simple constant in pre-Columbian history. It is the distinguishing mark of the civilization. Indeed, the extent of the Mexican people's evolution is dramatically illustrated by the development of their buildings.

Variety of styles and typology

While architecture enables us to measure the wider cultural areas, it also gives us a remarkable means of understanding and analyzing the astonishing artistic and cultural variety of Mexico. Middle America was not any more homogeneous than, for example, Europe; civilizations succeeded and were juxtaposed with one another in clearly defined areas, resulting in very different styles – important in that they determine the geographical extent of each civilization.

The varied typology is also important, because Middle America offers – apart from the omnipresent pyramid, whose plans vary, too – a whole range of buildings: temples, palaces, sportsgrounds, steam baths, fortifications, observatories, tombs, acropoli and innumerable urban developments.

New chronological criteria

We must know how to interpret traces of pre-Columbian sites. Excavation may give us the outline of the whole, but it does not tell us the dates of the individual constructions; and here stratigraphy can only hint at chronology. In order to place the principal centers in their historical context, to determine a stream of influences, we must know a building's age. In this domain, recent and far-reaching developments have upset all earlier theories.

During the last ten years, the extraordinarily rapid progress of archeological information about the pre-Columbian world has largely rendered worthless previous hypotheses on ancient Mexican civilizations. Datings made with Carbon 14 have disproved earlier theories; tentative suppositions, however ingenuous, have been supplanted by precise chronological data. Nonetheless, we still have to estimate how these earlier suppositions rank in importance. Perfection of research by radioactive means now enables us to obtain data that is reliable within a given margin of error. Yet archeology in Mexico has progressed, not only in research techniques, but also in the number of excavations carried out.

Recent discoveries

Scientific information has done much to cast new light on more than one civilization of the high plateaux or the Gulf of Mexico. We should note in particular the extensive excavations and reconstructions made at Teotihuacan (1962–1964), and the discoveries at Tlatelolco-Nonoalco (1963), in the very heart of the Mexican capital. This new information contributes much to our knowledge of the Mexican past; it enables us to reassess past discoveries and so obtain a fresh appraisal of ancient Mexican history. As a result, many aspects of pre-Columbian architecture will be simplified.

It is still too early to give a complete and exact picture of the Mexican peoples. It would be naive to suppose that we know enough at this stage to establish a definitive history. In fact, digging in Mexico has been going on only for some sixty years, whereas in Egypt, for example, the first excavations began a hundred and fifty years ago. Whole areas of the Central American past before the Conquest are still in shadow – even in darkness. If we consider that on Mexican territory alone some 11,000 archeological sites have been counted, we get some idea of the gaps in our knowledge; this becomes still more apparent when we realize that only fifty or sixty cities have been scientifically excavated.

Yet, considering the depths of uncertainty in which the past generation of archeologists were plunged, the latest discoveries reveal considerable progress. They enable us to draw up a balance-sheet – provisional, understandably – useful for anyone attempting to assess the historical evolution of the principal Indian cultures in Central America.

'Maya' and 'Ancient Mexico'

This book therefore considers not only entirely new material on recently excavated buildings – such as the Causeway of the Dead, the Square of the Moon and the palace of Quetzalpapalotl at Teotihuacan, the Pyramid of Santa Cecilia, the sacrificial center of Tlatelolco, the city of Yagul and buildings at Xochicalco – but also aims at giving pre-Columbian architecture an interpretation based on current historical and chronological data.

The overall subject of this book is the art of building in the principal pre-Columbian civilizations of Mexico. An earlier volume, 'Maya', dealt with building in Guatemala, Honduras and Yucatan between the 4th and 13th centuries A.D. We said there that the Mayans were the Greeks of the New World, but it does not necessarily follow that other pre-Columbian civilizations are any the less interesting.

We have, in fact, dissociated Mayan architecture from that of other Mexican civilizations because of fundamental differences. Mayan temples and palaces are characterized by a system of roofing unique in the Amerindic regions: only Mayans employed a false masonry vault that enabled them to roof their buildings with a mixture of stone embedded in cement. This feature explains why many more Mayan than other Central American constructions have survived. Mayan architecture holds a very special place in pre-Columbian culture not only because of numerous remains but also because of its differing styles and the complexity of its architectural plans.

We will not, in this book, return to the subject of Mayan construction; but we will refer to the influences and to the spread of population that led up Mayan architecture. It is indeed impossible to assess pre-Columbian architecture without referring to one of its principal exponents – one that unquestionably casts light on all parallel and earlier cultures.

Aims and outlines

Seven or eight civilizations, in addition to the Mayans, created outstanding forms of architecture. It is with these that we propose to deal: the Olmecs – the great founders – the Teotihuacans, the Zapotecs, the Totonacs, the Toltecs, the Mixtecs and the Aztecs, the Chichimecs and the inhabitants of Xochicalco. This survey covers the region extending from the Central Meseta (the high plateaux) to the shores of the Gulf of Mexico, and includes Oaxaca in central Mexico. It deals with the period between the 9th century B.C. and the 16th century A.D. We have thus to assess two and a half thousand years of architecture.

Although there is always some cultural unity, the marked differences in pre-Columbian methods of construction force us to analyze each system separately; we cannot group in one chapter a morphological, technological and functional survey of Central Mexico. Inevitably this will lead to some repetition, but it will result in a more explicit appraisal.

In order to emphasize the fundamental unity of the pre-Columbian world, we have devoted Chapter 1 to common cultural backgrounds from which later civilizations deviated. Chapter 2, dealing with current chronological data, explains the historical evolution of each of the principal cultural centers; it highlights their interaction, and evaluates archaic architectural theories.

Chapter 3 deals with the northern region and its capital, Teotihuacan. This great religious metropolis characterizes the advanced level reached by pre-Columbian culture two thousand years ago.

In Chapter 4, we will consider the city of Monte Alban, creation of the Zapotecs, together with the cities of Yagul and Mitla, capital of the Mixtecs; a natural connexion exists between the cultures of the Oaxaca region. This chapter also deals with the capital of the Totonacs, Tajin, on the Gulf of Mexico. Finally, in Chapter 5, we turn to the high plateaux of the Central Meseta to study the development of cultures stemming from Teotihuacan: Xochicalco, Tula, the Chichimecs and the Aztecs.

In conclusion, we will sum up pre-Columbian architecture in order to evaluate the contributions it made to the history of art.

At the dawn of the first great Middle American civilizations the inhabitants of the American continent were divided into two distinct groups. The nomads, who lived by hunting and fishing and who occupied most of the territory, were directly descended from the late Paleolithic age. The second group, who settled in temperate regions, had a neolithic way of life – agriculture, the domestication of animals, and the manufacture of ceramics. A mutual and deep-rooted hostility existed between the groups.

Distribution of population

Nomad territory extended from Alaska to North Mexico, an area of more than 10 million square miles. Their ancestors had been the first tribes to arrive in the New World, about 32,000 to 35,000 years ago. Originally from Asia, they reached the continent hunting animals over the solidly frozen waters of the Behring Straits – it is still possible at certain times of the year to cross from one continent to the other. The distance covered, some 50 miles, presented no problems for these early hunters.

The appearance of man in the New World is recent, compared to the 600,000 to a million years he is belived to have existed in Asia or Africa. However, the newcomers soon spread over the whole American continent; human remains discovered in Tierra del Fuego are apparently as old as those found in Canada.

The prehistoric American world was a very different place from that discovered by the first Conquistadores. By the sixteenth century no large animals existed (the Spaniards introduced the horse, cows and bulls), but five thousand years earlier the continent was still infested with mammoths and mastodons, wild horses, camels and giant sloths, cave bear, bison and wolves. During the neolithic age these species, with the exception of the last three, became extinct. Was this a result of over-intensive hunting? Did the climate, together with the disappearance of natural fauna, force man to modify his way of life, and transform him from paleolithic hunter into neolithic farmer?

The neolithic age

Considering that the neolithic age in the Middle East began some 10,000 years ago, its appearance on the American continent is, by prehistoric standards, recent; indeed, the 'conquest' of the American Far West during the eighteenth and nineteenth centuries may have been the Indians' final, desperate attempt to defend their traditional hunting grounds against encroaching settlers – in this case, the Whites.

The neolithic age was man's greatest step forward, and we may well wonder where the American neolithic period originated. From its inception in the Middle East, it spread over the globe, yet only reached the New World about five thousand years ago. Why? Did it take so long for the discoveries of the Old World to reach America? Or were contacts between Asiatic and American peoples made after the great Wisconsin ice-age? Highly contradictory theories have been advanced: some suggest a world-wide diffusion of the fundamental discoveries of man while others support simultaneous and multiple origins of knowledge.

One theory believes that material or religious connections imply the existence of contacts, lasting until the height of pre-Columbian civilizations, between the inhabitants of south-east Asia, Java and China, and those of the New World. The opposition claims that these connections are only accidental; each part of the world progressed independently, according to individual needs and circumstances.

The controversy does not really concern us here; it has been going on for fifty, if not a hundred years. The early explorers of the high plateaux and Yucatan dismissed the possibility of pre-Columbian civilizations having been indigenous; they advanced various theories: the migration of some lost tribe of Israel, the existence of Atlantis, the influence of Egypt and Mesopotamia.

While there is some evidence for this, and while there is also an interesting possibility that inter-continental contacts existed in the form of trade and ideology, none the less there are marked gaps in pre-Columbian cultures which would suggest that such connections were only sporadic, if not accidental. How otherwise can we explain the absence not only of animals but, above all, of flora such as cereals? Neither wheat nor rice were cultivated by pre-Columbians. Why? Did the Middle Americans prefer a religious society and architectural forms to agriculture and the development of a plant that would ensure the survival of the masses?

Pre-Columbian agriculture

Maize was the staple crop in the New World. For five thousand years settlers grew a type of maize with ears as thick as a finger; by hybridization and selection, this was to become the chief source of food for the pre-Columbians.

Additional crops included the black bean and calabash, which were cultivated in the fourth millennium (as has been shown by Carbon 14); and, later, the 'chile' or pepper, sweet potato, and avocado pear. The early Mexicans also grew tobacco, cotton, cocoa and 'maguey,' or American aloe, which produces 'pulque,' a sweet, whitish, fermented drink, rich in proteins. Fruits included the tomato, guava, papaya and, later, the pineapple.

The origins of these crops is interesting: connections had apparently existed between the north and south continents. The large-grain type of maize seems to have been grown first in the Andean regions, while cotton first appeared in Peru. The connections become more intriguing when we consider the origins of pre-Columbian metallurgy. Certainly long-established commercial relations existed between the Middle American and Andean cultures, and this is not surprising since the early nomadic tribes had traveled through Middle America on their way south. It was in these forested regions that the first Mexican civilization, the Olmecs, was to flourish.

Pre-Columbian methods of agriculture were extremely primitive: the plough did not exist and the Indian's only implement was a kind of digging stick. Because there were no cereals, the system of monoculture was unknown; several crops were sown simultaneously in one field. The soil undeniably benefited from this method – it needed less rotation and remained fertile – and labor was, moreover, fully exploited.

Technological background

The inhabitants of Middle America were not, apparently, preoccupied with the requirements of everyday life. The wheel, one of the basic discoveries of man, never existed, although the huge buildings necessitated the transport of heavy materials. The Indian's ingenuity was reserved for his leisure and was never applied for purely functional purposes. There is no evidence of the potter's wheel, despite the exceptionally important role of ceramics both in Mexico and Peru.

To the end, pre-Columbian civilizations employed a neolithic form of tool. They never really advanced beyond the stage of the polished or sharpened stone. Tools were usually made of flint or obsidian. Grindstones of hard stone, mallets and pestles of diorite and basalt were to remain in use until the pre-Columbian world ceased to exist.

Metallurgy – developed only about 1000 A. D. – never influenced the manufacture of tools; copper and, even more so, gold and silver, were reserved for decorative purposes. Jewelry, however, reveals very advanced techniques: wire-drawing, riveting, soldering, etc.

Pre-Columbian jewelers at this period worked with precious and semi-precious stones such as turquoise, jade, rock crystal, amethyst, onyx, agate, chalcedony and sardonyx. The feathers of the quetzal bird were also in great demand for decorating ceremonial robes.

We must not, however, give the term 'neolithic' too narrow a meaning; nor should we compare it with the neolithic age of very ancient civilizations. There are considerable differences between the stone-age civilizations of the Old and New Worlds. In Europe and the Middle East neolithic or bronze-age tribes owned herds and beasts of burden. In America, apart from the dog, the only domestic animals were bees, turkeys and, in Andean regions, the llama.

Stone-age pre-Columbians were, nevertheless, the builders of great stone and mortar cities. Their hieroglyphics provided an adequate system for writing and numerals. It is worth noting that writing in the Old World, unlike Middle America, usually developed after metallurgy. In Mexico, however, writing coexisted with architecture, and both were to find their fullest expression in Mayan civilization.

Pre-Columbians had a complex calendar and system of calculation. Their knowledge of mathematics and astronomy was remarkable. At the time of the Conquest, 1200 medicinal plants were listed, and Aztec surgeons were accustomed to set fractures, practised dentistry and even performed trepanning operations. The Aztecs must have inherited all this from their ancestors, for it is unlikely that such advanced discoveries were made at this period. The connotation of the term 'neolithic,' when applied to the Old and New Worlds, is therefore very different.

Physical features

Although they had neolithic backgrounds in common pre-Columbian civilizations did not develop simultaneously. The transformation from a nomadic to a settled existence is indicated by agriculture, but, up to the time of the Conquest, sedentary tribes occupied a relatively small area of the continent. Over 10,000,000 square miles of North and Central America belonged to the nomads, whereas cultivated land covered an area of only 585,000 square miles—some twenty time less. Yet this small area was to be the home of numerous Middle American cultures.

This is largely explained by Mexico's physical and climatic features. Few countries offer such marked contrasts: the horn-shaped land is characterized by differences in climate resulting from extreme variations in altitude.

The Gulf of Mexico has a sub-tropical climate, hot and humid. Rainfall is heavy, and Amazonian-type jungle covers the region; trees are often 90 to 120 feet high. The undergrowth harbors jaguars, hog and deer, and the rivers are infested with alligators. The extensive coastal plain, often flooded, is cut off from the sea by a chain of lagoons: sometimes land and water seem to merge. Here we find the states of Tabasco, Veracruz and Tamaulipas; Chiapas is almost totally overgrown with jungle.

Having left the jungle for the upper regions of central Mexico, we encounter a completely different country. Although still green, the soil has clearly been affected by tellurian movement; the lowland jungles are replaced by conifers; prairies give way to foothills, then tortuous mountains and steep valleys through which shallow streams cut a way to the sea.

In the distance are the perennial snows blanketing mountains which include Orizaba (17,000 feet), and Popocateptl. Beyond this barrier are the high plateaux of the Central Meseta. Situated at a height of 6000 and 7000 feet, the plateaux are encircled by icy

The region of Mexico

Maps of ancient Mexico

1	Tepotzotlan	12	Teayo
2	Ticoman	13	Cempoala
3	El Arbolillo	14	Tres Zapotes
4	Zacatenco	15	La Venta
5	Tenochtitlan	16	Palenque
6	Copilco	17	Uxmal
7	Cuicuilco	18	Chichen Itza
8	Xochimilco	19	Tikal
9	Tepoztlan	20	Kaminaljuyu
10	Teopanzolco	21	Copan
11	Cholula		

The Lake of Texcoco as it was at the time of Cortez.
All the sites named on the maps are illustrated in the plates.

peaks and extinct volcanoes. The climate is temperate and, apart from summer, rainfall is moderate. The plateaux were once densely forested but for the last thousand years intensive felling of trees has transformed them into a cruelly eroded region, with extensive arid areas interrupted by meager strips of fertile land.

The western slopes that descend to the Pacific also have forested regions, and a central cultivated strip. Mexico is bounded by the jungle to the South, and by the extensive deserts or semi-deserts of Sonora and Chihuaha to the North; they form a kind of natural frontier for the regions in which the early civilizations flourished.

Numerous homogeneous civilizations

The striking physical contrasts of Mexico account for the many different forms of culture. Climate, isolated valleys and coastal plains, regions often separated by tropical jungle—all encouraged variety. Much as European centers were responsible for different art forms, so the Mexican world gave birth to independent cultures. Although the variations from the common background are more noticeable than in Europe, their increase was prevented by technological limitations. Yet this background did give pre-Columbian civilizations cohesion, both in religion and art.

That a unity of religious beliefs existed is clearly indicated by the forms and names of the divinities. Rites are similar almost everywhere, and stem from the two basic divinities, sun and rain, together with a highly complex pantheistic system.

Architecture, a unifying element

Because of the religious unity, the functions of sacred buildings were similar, and the architectonic types of all regions were closely related. The common denominator is therefore to be found in an architectural homogeneity that, despite the existence of individual styles, characterizes all major constructions.

The pyramid is a primary constant in Middle American civilizations. Places of worship everywhere assume the form of artificial or natural eminences, whose function is to support the actual sanctuaries or temples. Unlike the Egyptian pyramid, which was never built to be climbed and was only a monumental tomb, the pre-Columbian pyramid had a staircase leading to a platform on which the sanctuary was erected. In this respect, the Mexican pyramid was more closely related to the Mesopotamian ziggurat. Some pyramids contained tombs, but in these cases they remained first and foremost temples – the funerary aspect never eclipsed the true function of the monument.

Another type of construction common to almost every advanced Middle American civilization is the ball-court. Its form varies, but it usually consists of a court in the shape of a flattened H with boundaries marked either by vertical walls or embankments. On each side of the center of the court two stone rings are fastened to the summit of the walls, about ten feet from the ground. The 'game' played in this open-air sportsground had a religious significance related to the course of the sun. A solid rubber ball weighing several pounds was used, and participants played not with their hands or feet but with forearms and hips.

The great Middle American cultures are therefore characterized by extremely original types of constructions which, because of their common origins, constitute a unifying element. It follows that pre-Columbian architecture is more than a distinctive form of plastic expression: it has a significant place in the history of mankind.

Early constructional techniques

Only stone buildings have survived the ravages of time, but although some regions are devoid of any constructions we must not infer that they were non-existent. Over a long period places of worship were, like peasant dwellings, built of perishable materials such as beaten earth, mud, wattle, thatch and wood. Even at the height of the classical period, masonry pyramids were often surmounted by sanctuaries of rough brick or wood, roofed with palm branches on a wooden framework.

Advanced pre-Columbian civilizations were using stone or limestone mortar about two thousand years ago. Indeed, limestone was employed to such an extent – whole pyramids were faced with a layer of stucco – that vast areas were completely denuded of trees. Wood was, in fact, the only combustible material used by pre-Columbians. Limestone was made by a very primitive method: logs and bundles of sticks were piled up in a circular heap about six feet high, on top of which were arranged pebbles of crushed limestone. In the absence of an 'oven' or kiln, the amount of wood burned was out of all proportion to the end-product.

The cities of the gods

What is most striking about Mexican architecture and town-planning is that, despite elementary techniques, it reveals an astonishing breadth of concept and sense of grandeur. The great sacred complexes of the theocratic cities were designed with mathematical precision; there was usually a master plan governing the establishment of large communities.

The systematic deployment of the sacred cities served to increase the significance of a hierarchical society, ruled by priest-kings and administered by sacred colleges. Perhaps a rather summary interpretation, it nevertheless is confirmed by the observations of the first Conquistadores. The absolute power of the Aztec lords at the time of the Spanish invasion suggests that pre-Columbians had always been ruled by a theocracy – at any rate in the great stone-built cities. History shows that cities built of 'hard materials' are usually theocracies.

On the other hand, the eminently lay aspect of ceramics from the west coast of Mexico, and the almost total lack of monumental architecture there, imply a different social system. It seems as though the development of a centralized authority was accompanied by a corresponding increase in the importance of architecture.

A parallel does exist between religion and the construction of large cities. Corporate life in those times had a common aim; it was based on shared beliefs and, consequently was expressed in similar ways and against a majestic background. Painting, sculpture and ceramics all reveal this unity. The ceramics of the Zapotecs – the foremost architects of central Mexico – consist primarily of funerary urns and figures of divinities, while the spontaneous and attractive scenes of daily life from western Pacific regions, such as Nayarit, Colima and Jalisco, characterize civilizations that, as far as we know, never constructed great sacred complexes – although their neighbors in La Quemada and Tzintzuntzan are noted for their colossal monuments.

The scale of town-planning seems to have been directly dependent on the social system, and the latter increased as religion became more important. This is a natural development in a society where all permanent buildings are dedicated to divinities and their acolytes. The purely religious function of architecture was fundamental to the pre-Columbian world – as in the great agrarian civilizations of Egypt and Mesopotamia.

We should not, however, give the term 'religious' too narrow an interpretation; a current and common mistake is to consider pre-Columbian architecture as consisting only of temples and sanctuaries, excluding palaces and living-quarters. In societies governed by a divine will, there can be no distinction between the gods and their representatives: priest-kings are basic to a theocracy, and they exercise their authority as much on the temporal as on the spiritual level. Consequently, the religious hierarchy of pre-Columbian civilizations lived in the temple area; and their palaces were built of stone, like the temples on which they were to a certain extent dependent. I have already proved this point in my book on Mayan architecture,* and it has since been confirmed by the discovery of the palace of Quetzalpapalotl at Teotihuacan.

Mayan palaces, along with those of other pre-Columbian civilizations, were not retreats. They were designed as the permanent living-quarters for priests and dignitaries, and their architectural style was therefore religious. The close association of palace and temple can be found throughout the pre-Columbian world.

Homogeneity in the Mexican world

Starting from identical rudimentary techniques, pre-Columbian architecture was and remained a unifying element in Middle America. Builders were therefore influenced by similar methods, and by a similar type and basic plan of construction. Despite local variations in style, pre-Columbian buildings are part of a widespread homogeneity.

As a result, it seems less arbitrary to devote only a few pages to some seven or eight types of architecture that evolved during 2500 years. Were it not for this similarity we should be in the invidious position of the historian who aims at evaluating in one volume all the buildings erected from the time of the Parthenon to contemporary Brasilia! Despite the number of Mexican civilizations, we can compare our position with the Egyptologist, who is faced with three thousand years of architecture. However, although we are closer in time to our subject, our knowledge and evaluation of the New World is nowhere near as great as that of the Pharaonic world.

Plates

Teotihuacan

21 The pyramid of the Sun seen from the air. Its five steps can be seen also the staircases leading to the sanctuary, of which only the foundations remain.

22 The north-west corner of the pyramid of the Sun.

23 The pyramid of the Sun seen from the Causeway of the Dead. The base of the stairs leading to the sanctuary consists of two flights situated on either side of the forepart. They come together at the second storey, separate at the third storey, and join to scale the vertical section and uppermost platform.

24 Aerial view of the pyramid of the Moon and the square encircled by platforms. In the background, the Causeway of the Dead, the pyramid of the Sun, and the Citadel.

25 The four-tiered platforms that surround the Square of the Moon. They were restored from 1962 to 1964.

26 The disciplined structures of the Square of the Moon.

27 The characteristic Teotihuacan 'tablero', or panel, with its frame surmounting a 45° mound.

28 The palace of Quetzalpapalotl: unique example of the analytical style as applied to a dwelling planned for priests and high dignitaries of the City of the Gods.

29 Details of bas-reliefs decorating the pillars of the palace of Quetzalpapalotl. At left, the Quetzal bird seen in profile. At right, the same symbol seen full-face, with a breastplate in the shape of a butterfly.

30 The palace of Quetzalpapalotl encircled by porticoed galleries surrrounding a broad patio. The rooms are very dimly lit, and open onto the gallery.

31 Frescoes decorate the raised 'benches' along the gallery. The symbolical jaguars are painted in white against a red background, with green and black highlights.

◀ Plans

32 Perspective of the Causeway of the Dead, following restoration.

33 The four platforms lining the western side of the Citadel, along the Causeway of the Dead. In the background, the pyramid of the Sun is outlined against the Cerro Gordo.

34–35 Staircases and platforms on the south wing of the Citadel. The sobriety of the plastic methods used is remarkable when compared to the effect of the platforms and steps bounding a 660 foot square.

36 The south side of the Citadel, seen from the great entrance staircase.

37 The square altar in the center of the quadrilateral.

38 A double staircase leading to one of the platforms that marks the boundary of the Citadel.

39 The staircases bordering the south side of the Citadel.

40 The principal staircase on the forepart of the temple of Quetzalcoatl. At left, the eastern staircase of the altar.

41 The monumental staircase of the first temple of Quetzalcoatl. The ramps are enlivened by the fierce jaws of the Plumed Serpent, sculpted in relief.

42 The temple of Quetzalcoatl: the façade decorated with freestone motifs was discovered beneath the masonry of the later forepart which preserved the earlier layer intact. The sculptures framed in the panels depict alternately masks of Tlaloc, god of rain, and heads of Plumed Serpents.

43 The motifs decorating the panels of the temple of Quetzalcoatl. Above, the head of a Plumed Serpent emerging from a 'solar' halo. Below, the geometrically stylized mask of Tlaloc.

44 In the foreground, the staircase of the temple of Quetzalcoatl, with a head of a Plumed Serpent emerging from the ramp. Middle ground, one of the Citadel platforms. In the background, the pyramid of the Sun, situated more than 4950 feet north of the Citadel, and outlined against the Cerro Gordo.

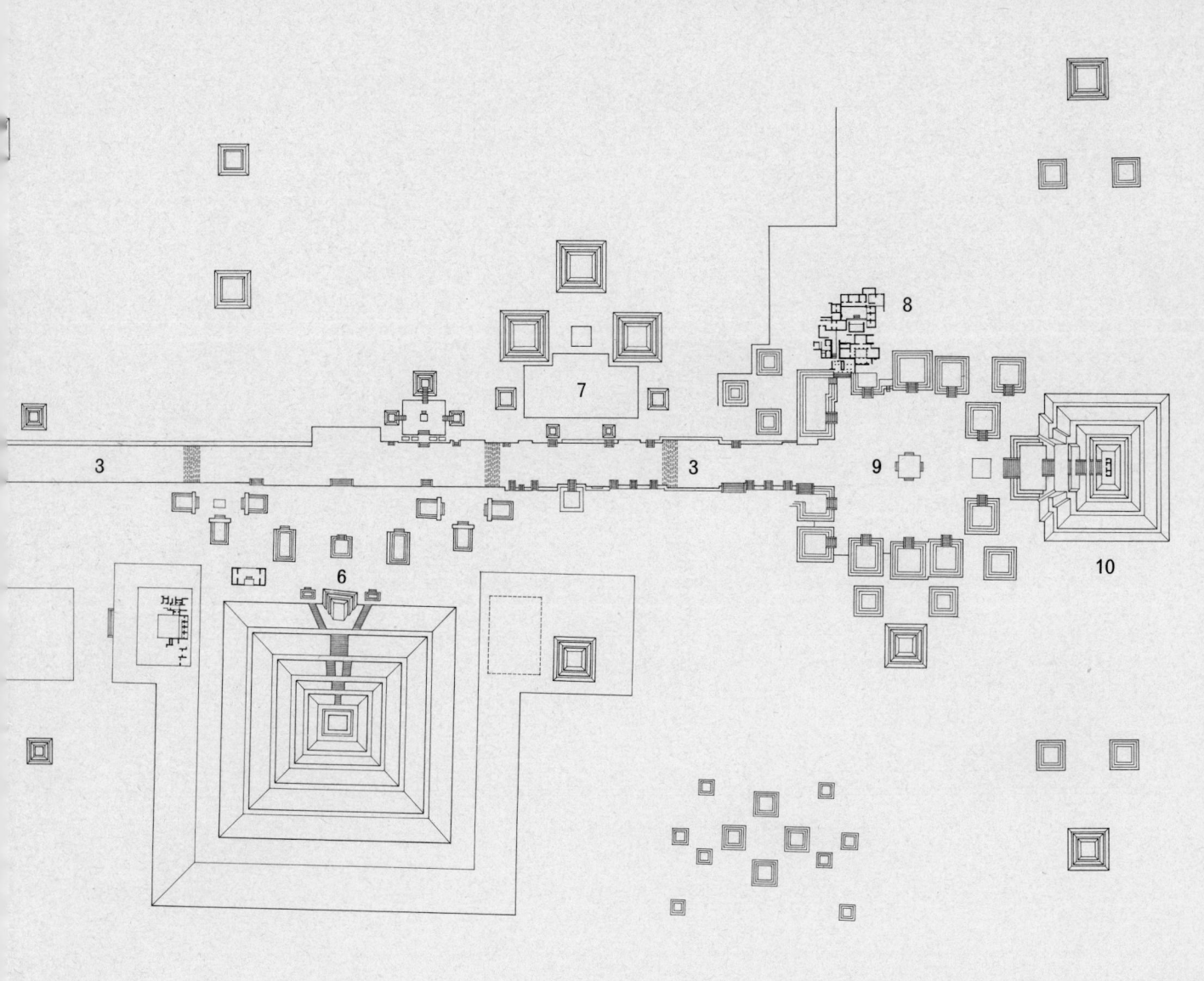

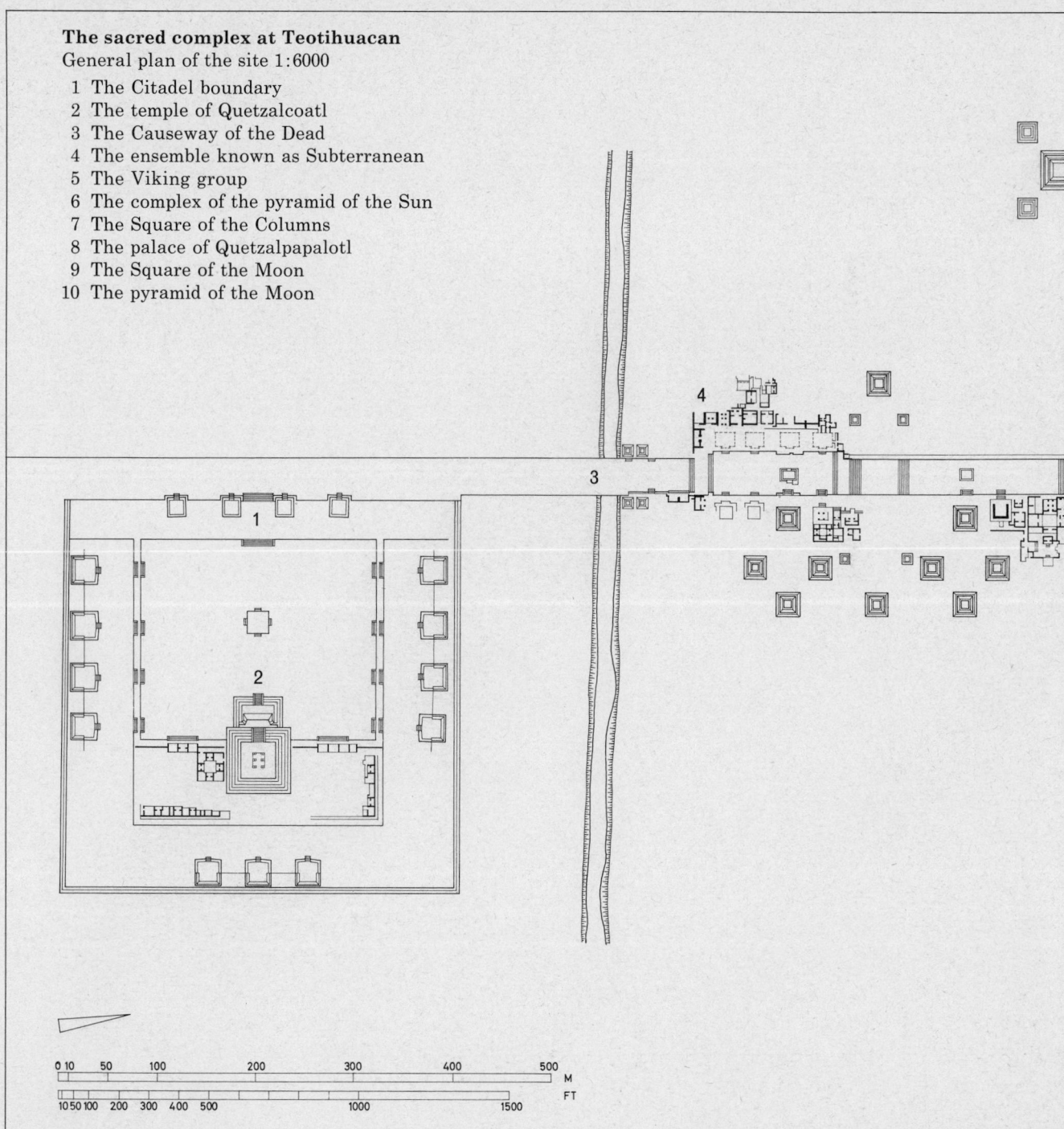

The sacred complex at Teotihuacan
General plan of the site 1:6000

1 The Citadel boundary
2 The temple of Quetzalcoatl
3 The Causeway of the Dead
4 The ensemble known as Subterranean
5 The Viking group
6 The complex of the pyramid of the Sun
7 The Square of the Columns
8 The palace of Quetzalpapalotl
9 The Square of the Moon
10 The pyramid of the Moon

Notes

Teotihuacan

The widespread excavations begun in 1962 at Teotihuacan by the Instituto Nacional de Antropologia e Historia of Mexico has considerably affected the former appearance of the city. It was a major undertaking: eight archeologists, fourteen assistants and 1500 workers, led by Professor Ignacio Bernal, Director of the Museo Nacional de Antropologia of Mexico. In two and a half years four principal tasks were achieved:
1. The reconstruction of buildings surrounding the Square of the Moon, including the front face of the pyramid of the Moon.
2. The restoration of the palace of Quetzalpaplotl and the civil buildings around it.
3. The excavation and restoration of the major part of platforms, quadrilaterals and staircases bordering the Causeway of the Dead.
4. The preservation and restoration of some hundred frescoes discovered during the course of excavation.

The Square of the Moon

Before the start of the 1962 excavations, the Square of the Moon was a series of shapeless mounds, covered by vegetation. However, no sooner had work begun than archeologists discovered the bases of staircases and the interior corners of several platforms, which enabled them to establish their exact plans and the number of superimposed steps. Gradually the huge complex was revealed. The method was the same as that used by Manuel Gamio some forty years earlier on the Citadel, but which was perfected here. The difficulties on this site were greater: for example in the reconstruction of a great staircase scaling the forepart of the pyramid of the Moon. The importance of the reconstructions may be judged by the remarkable number of places where the original layers have been preserved: these undoubtedly show that the outer 'skin' of the monument has been found. Furthermore, areas that had to be filled up have been clearly shown, by means of small stones scattered in the modern cement.

The palace of Quetzalpapalotl

Still more difficult and delicate an operation was the restoration of the palace of Quetzalpapalotl. Although the building which flanks one of the platforms to the southwest of the Square of the Moon was intentionally destroyed during the 5th-century invasions, none the less fairly numerous remains survived and enabled its total restoration. The pillars lining the patio were not made of masonry, as in most of the priests' dwellings at Teotihuacan, but of large, carefully dressed blocks, decorated with magnificent bas-reliefs. The twelve pillars all had the same motifs: butterfly and Quetzal bird. Consequently, whenever parts of this ornamentation were discovered—and some pillars were almost intact—it was possible to identify each fragment and place it in its correct position. This task was made easier by the fact that the reliefs had been carved after the blocks were set up. Thus each block could only fit one place. The integrity of the works is again visible in the method of restoration: missing blocks were replaced by modern versions, sculpted with similar motifs; but each modern block is distinguished by fine vertical lines.

Numerous frescoes came to light during excavations in the palace area. Those along the patios and galleries were left in situ. The others were detached by methods already proved successful with Catalonian Roman frescoes and Etruscan paintings. Having been removed from their original position—often almost ruined—or even rescued in fragments from the ruins, the frescoes were transferred onto rigid metal frames, then patiently cleaned and restored. The result is a remarkable documentation of the religious and everyday life of the Teotihuacans.

The Causeway of the Dead

From the pyramid of the Moon to the face of the pyramid of the Sun, near the Viking Group were numerous platforms and ensembles, consisting of squares surrounded by buildings and staircases. All of these have been reconstructed. The Causeway of the Dead at Teotihuacan has thus rediscovered its former splendor, and the impressive perspective of this 1¼ mile-long ceremonial avenue gives an idea of how the City of the Gods must have appeared.

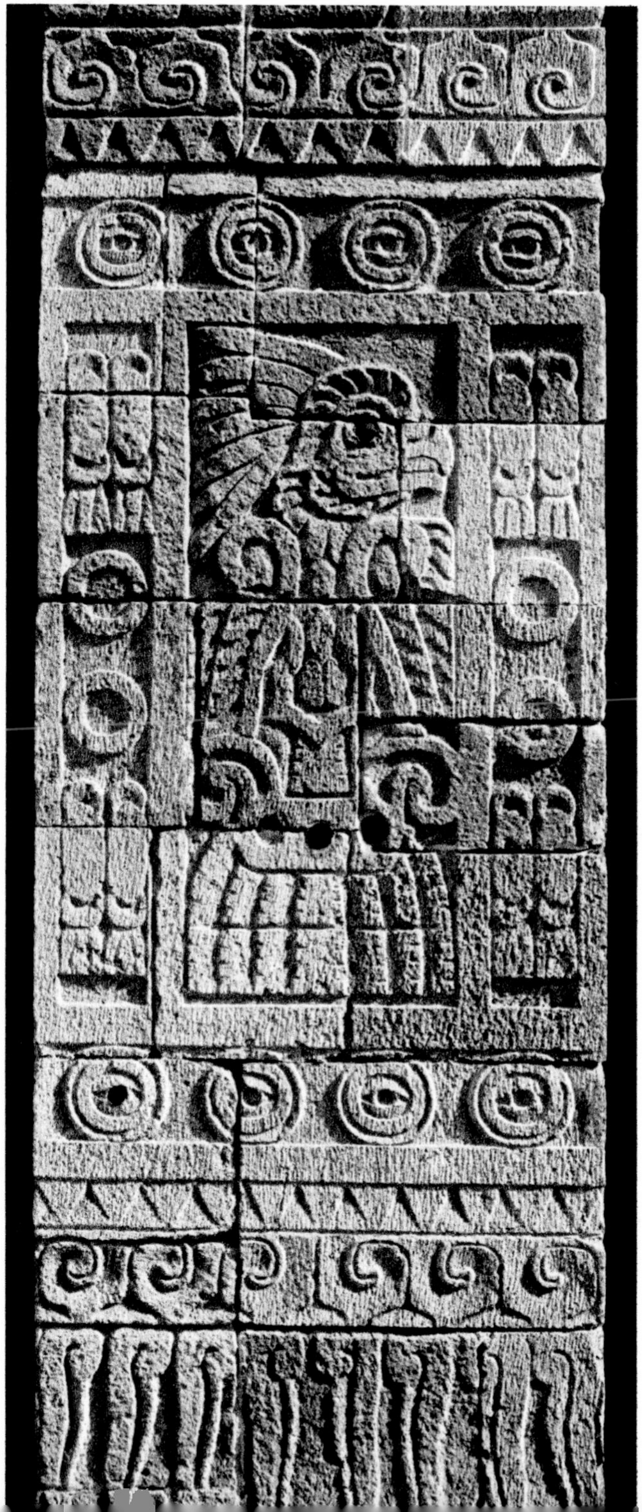

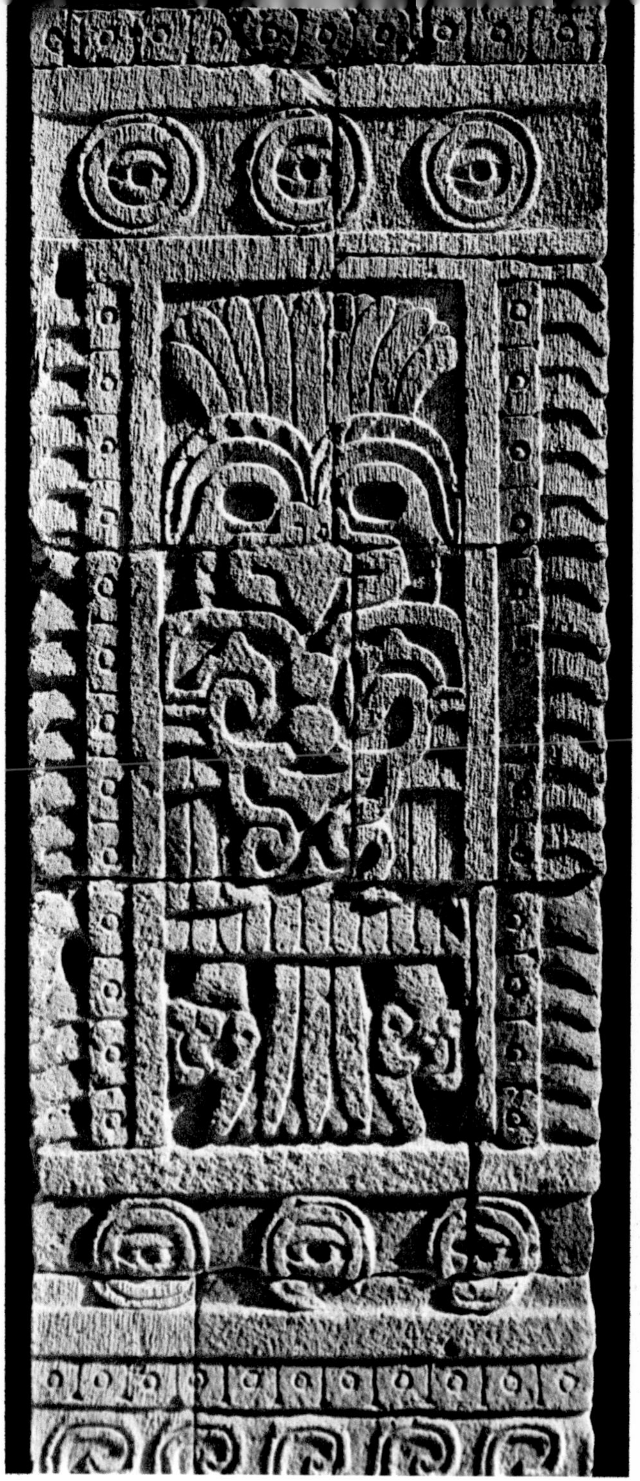

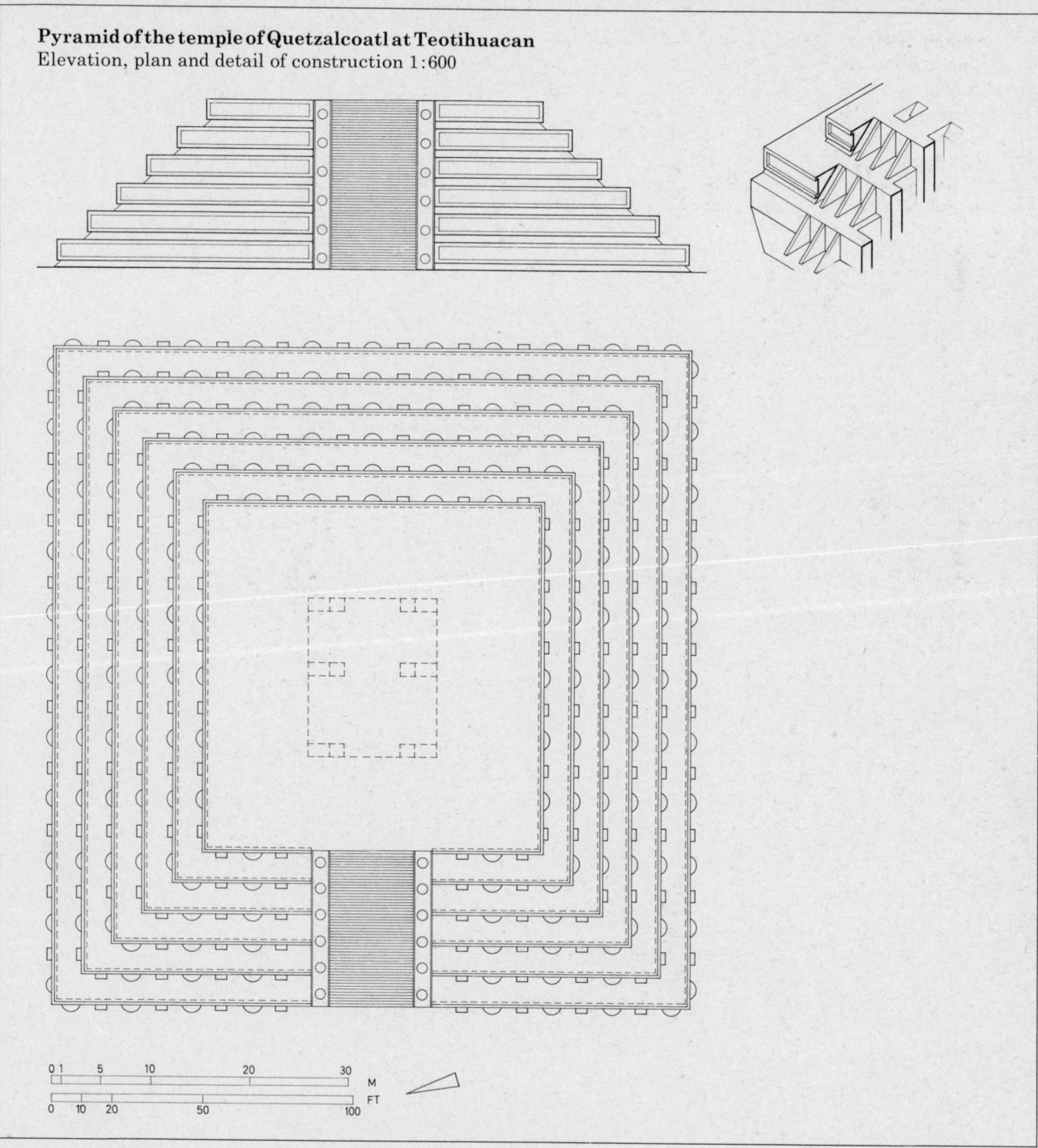

Pyramid of the temple of Quetzalcoatl at Teotihuacan
Elevation, plan and detail of construction 1:600

0 1   5   10   20   30   M
0   10   20   50   100   FT

Palace of Quetzalpapalotl at Teotihuacan

Plan and section 1:400

1 The hypostyle hall linking the Square of the Moon
   with the palace
2 The patio surrounded by galleries with porticoes on
   pillars
3 Rooms used as living quarters
4 Site of a platform in the Square of the Moon

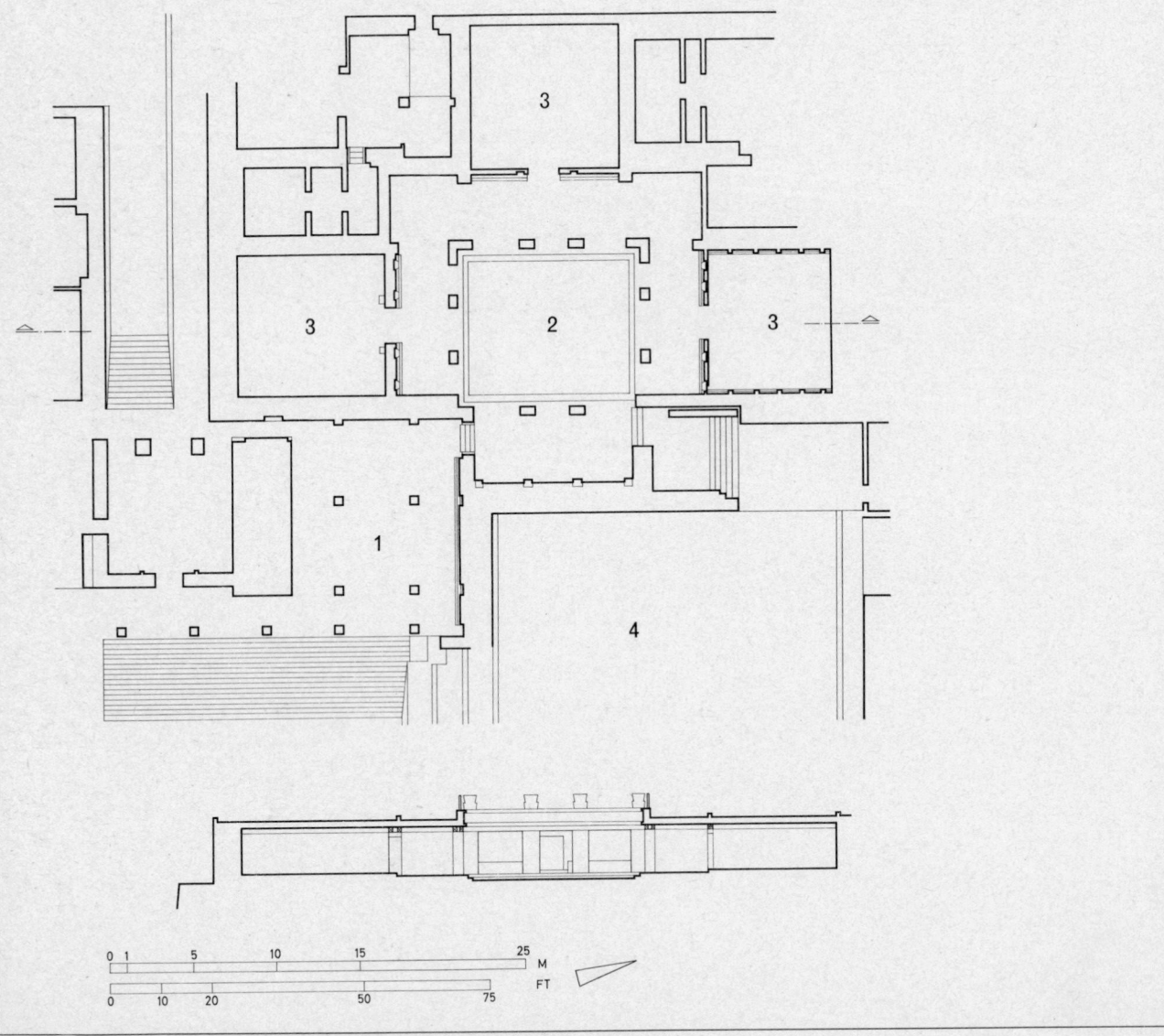

0 1   5   10   15   25 M
0   10   20   50   75 FT

2. The Birth of architecture

The mystery surrounding the pre-Columbian world derives largely from the scarcity of documented evidence and the difficulty in deciphering what there is. Although a few Mexican civilizations possessed systems of writing and numerics – some even dated their monuments – the systems are for the most part undecipherable and therefore of no value. Even Mayan records, extensive as they are, have proved unsatisfactory, for the greatest problem consists in establishing a concordance between Mayan and contemporary systems of calculation. In short, we still cannot determine the precise equivalent of a Mayan date, and suggestions for a date can vary between one hundred and two hundred and fifty years. The Mayan civilization existed from the beginning of the Christian era until the 13th century, so the variations are obviously unacceptable to any historian accustomed to the chronology of the Old World which, for the past thirty years, has generally been exact.

Early Mexican civilizations are even more difficult to date; few, if any, inscriptions are extant. What has been established merely complicates the issue. For example, we have still to determine whether the Olmec's system of dating corresponds to that of the Mayans, the Zapotecs (which so far defies all analysis), the Totonacs, or the inhabitants of Xochicalco; and in many cases information based on excavations is too inexact to provide a key to chronology.

Until recently, attempts to establish a chronology therefore followed a similar pattern: monuments were freely dated, some too early and others too late. For the last twenty years, however, there have been marked efforts to coordinate the various chronologies of Middle American civilizations. Outstanding among those who have advanced theories on comparative chronology are: Thompson, Zimmerman, A. Caso, W. Andrews, R. Smith, Jimenez Moreno, S. Borhegyi, H. Boggs, G. Payon, A. Medellin, G. Lowe and A. Mason, J. Paddock, and R. Pina Chan. Pina Chan recently published a plan which coordinates the various systems. Although contemporary hypotheses should be considered with some reservation, and will undoubtedly require modification (in this book I purposely adopt early datings), results have none the less proved encouraging. Successive theories are at last beginning to converge and, moreover, historical localization of different ancient Mexican cultures is becoming increasingly accurate.

Stratigraphy and 'indicative sherds'

Until now, no one date has been definitely established, no one landmark unreservedly accepted. Scientific research is not at fault for, at best, it can only advance possibilities. Hypotheses are based primarily on stratigraphy and ceramics. Archeologists examining a site first attempt to determine in which strata remains have been unearthed. Neolithic and subsequent strata most often yield pottery fragments – pottery is virtually indestructible.

Every age produces some form of pottery – containers, vases, statuary – and the forms and ornamentation often typify a particular period. When clearly identifiable fragments are discovered in a layer (which is itself related to a pre-determined architectural style) it becomes possible to connect the layer with a definite period; we know that the civilization it represents precedes and follows a previously determined strata. Furthermore, if identical remains are discovered on another site it follows that the two layers are contemporary. Archeologists refer to these fragments as 'indicative sherds', and the relative chronology they provide is extremely interesting. They enable us to establish not so much the precise date of a civilization as the successive periods; and sites often at great distances from one another are shown to be contemporary. From a historical viewpoint this may seem somewhat vague, but archeologically it has proved very valuable.

Carbon 14

Although we may not be able to establish the exact date of a civilization by relating it to its predecessors we do know something about its age. Over the last fifteen years archeologists have used a new method in determining the age of a site: analysis of the radioactive organic remains.

Recent progress in the field of atomics and physics has provided specialists with a remarkable means of investigation; and although first results were marred by errors in application, so casting doubts on its efficacy, today the process is astonishingly accurate. It is known as Carbon 14, and can determine the age of every organic remain – charcoal, cloth, bones, etc.

The Carbon 14 process may be briefly explained as follows: during their existence all live organisms assimilate carbon. A small part of this is radioactive, and is called Carbon 14 (after its atomic weight); it is always present in living tissues. The assimilation ceases when the organisms die; Carbon 14 then begins to be discharged, losing radiating energy. The process can be compared to that of a battery. Because the loss is regular, and the amount of Carbon 14 in a living organism is also constant and equal to that present in the atmosphere, it is possible, given the rate of radiation at the time of analysis, to establish the age of the object under observation. The amount of Carbon 14 discharged is halved every 5570 years; for example, after 11,140 years only one quarter of the original amount – equivalent to that in the atmosphere – is left.

Archeology is, in this way, provided with an atomic 'clock' which gives the 'time' of organic remains; these in turn are related to the strata in which they were discovered. However, errors are possible and must be taken into account; and methods of analysis – carbonization, or transformation into gaseous states – together with the sensitivity of the instruments, can cause variations. Consequently, results sometimes vary from 50, 100, 150 to 200 and even 300 years. Furthermore, experiments have to be repeated until inaccuracies are eliminated and a statistical figure established. Only in this way can scientific results be obtained.

Radical changes in chronology

The results of these methods, when applied to Middle American remains, exceeded all expectations; indeed every hitherto accepted theory was rejected.

The Olmecs (the name means 'inhabitant of the rubber country'), one of the earliest and least known pre-Columbian civilizations, provide a striking example of this. The first Olmec site to be excavated, between 1938 and 1940, was at La Venta, in the state of Tabasco near the Gulf of Mexico; until then Olmec remains had consisted only of a few finely executed sculptures. The diggings were directed by Matthew W. Stirling, and brought to light remarkable remains. La Venta is built on a neck of marshy land bordering the river Tonala; buried deep in the jungle, it is surrounded by a network of lagoons and shallow streams, and is therefore almost inaccessible. Yet colossal stone monuments were unearthed on this site.

They consisted of monolithic statues in the form of altars, several cubic feet in size, stelae in relief, enormous plaster human heads, and smaller jade objects in the same style.

Until 1955, when a colleague of Stirling recommenced work on the site, the Olmec remains were generally dated between 150 B.C. and 800 A.D., because of the extremely ancient aspect of Olmec culture. The earliest evidence of Olmec art, dated some hundred years before Christ, was believed to be contemporary with the rise of Teotihuacan and Monte Alban. There was also controversy over the true center of Middle American civilizations: was it the high plateaux, the Gulf of Mexico, the mountains, or the shores of the Pacific?

The results of Drucker's work at La Venta have proved all earlier theories incorrect. Olmec remains at La Venta are much older than anyone suspected. Carbon 14 has shown that Olmec monuments at La Venta and Tres Zapotes date from about the 9th century B.C.; the sites were destroyed respectively about 400 B.C. and 175 B.C. The first pre-Columbian cultures existed, therefore, seven hundred years earlier than had been generally believed – a remarkable difference!

The Olmecs and the development of the classical period

The new evaluation gains added significance when we remember that the Olmecs created the earliest known monumental architecture, and were also the initiators of the groups of sacred buildings that characterized all pre-Columbian cultures until the sixteenth century. Like Minerva rising fully armed from the head of Jupiter, the impact of the Olmec civilization on history was immediate.

However, we should not take this metaphor too literally: a sacred city is not built in a few years, nor even in a few centuries! Carbon 14 has shown that the earliest city communities of Middle America date from about 1500 B.C. (Tlalilco) and 1200 B.C. (Kaminaljuyu); but these are pre-classical civilizations. The Olmecs' pre-classical period began during the 15th century B.C. However, a proto-classic civilization existed at La Venta and Tres Zapotes from the 9th century onwards, as is proved by the existence both of an advanced form of sculpture and by colossal architectural monuments.

Thenceforward, Olmec culture reveals almost all the characteristics common to great Middle American civilizations: ceremonial centers, stone sculpture, and a form of worship that was to be perpetuated until the demise of the pre-Columbian world.

Birth of architecture

Almost isolated from the mainland by swamps and tropical jungle, and with an unhealthy climate, La Venta was nevertheless the first great sacred city in the New World, and its architecture included all the principal types of pre-Columbian buildings.

Perhaps the most striking construction is the enormous rectangular-shaped pyramid of beaten earth, with a base consisting of two juxtaposed squares. It measures 429 feet long by 214.5 feet wide; rising to a height of 115.5 feet, its angle of elevation is approximately 30 degrees on the north and south faces. The upper platform (39.6 feet square), which once supported a sanctuary built of wood and thatch, is reached by the shallowest slopes of the pyramid.

The dimensions of the pyramid – three million cubic feet in volume, more than 200,000 tons of material – illustrate the Olmecs' remarkable breadth of concept. It is flanked by a number of buildings, arranged on a strict north-south axis, whose maximum deviation is only about eight degrees.

North of the pyramid and exactly in line with its longer sides are two parallel mounds, 280.5 feet by 52.8 feet, and about 20 feet high. This enclosure is possibly the earliest known ballcourt in Middle America. It is large for a court of this period, and is similar to the ballcourts discovered at Chichen Itza, Yucatan and Tajin.

The Olmecs were probably also the originators of the game, played with solid rubber balls weighing several pounds. The species of tree ('havea') from which the latex was obtained grows only in the Mexican jungle.

North of the ballcourt is a large quadrilateral, surrounded by an embankment on which stand rows of connecting basalt pillars. Within the quadrilateral is a roughly rectangular square. Two platforms form a link with the ballcourt. Crowds probably watched the ceremonies from this square.

Subsequently, two large circular mounds were constructed on the axis of the group, one situated in the northern part of the ballcourt, the other north of the quadrilateral. Each of the mounds contained a tomb, and their function was similar to that of tombs later discovered at Monte Alban. Sacred areas were venerated long after they had, for practical purposes, been abandoned, and rulers considered it an honor to be buried there.

Undoubtedly, then, La Venta was a major sacred

Plan of the site of La Venta. 1 Tumulus with tomb. 2 Large quadrilateral. 3 Tumulus with tomb. 4 Ballcourt bounded by two mounds 280.5 feet long. 5 Earth pyramid measuring 429 feet by 214.5 feet

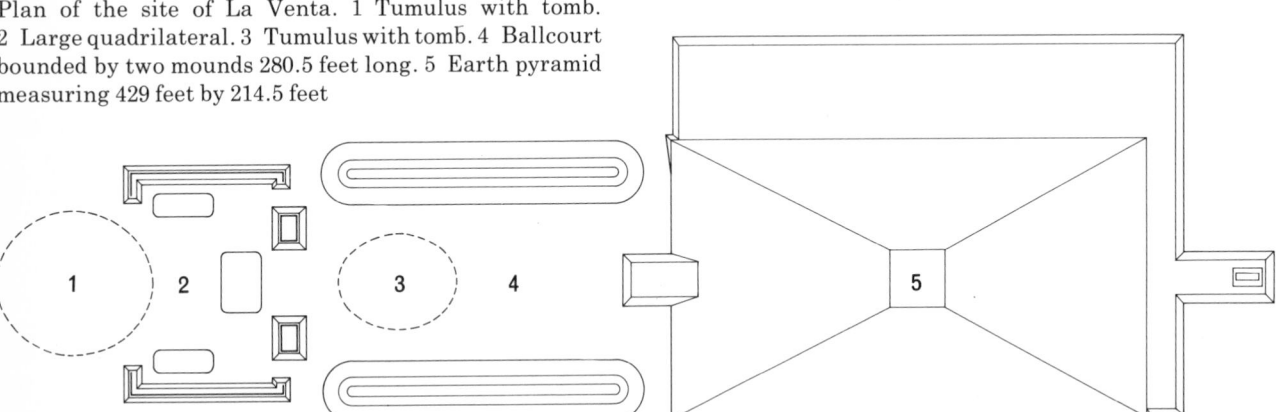

center, and it covered an area of more than 1000 by 270 feet. Although constructed chiefly of beaten earth, its buildings required an enormous amount of material and labor. We can gain some idea of the vast scale of the operation by assuming that every laborer made six journeys a day carrying a load of 77 lbs each time, a total of 450 lbs. Allowing for the rainy season when little or no work was done, this means that 1000 laborers would have taken five years to construct the pyramid. Furthermore, this number is only representative: in actual fact the total number of laborers must have been four or five times greater. Extra food and lodgings had to be provided by the community. All this indicates that during the construction of the great pyramid, La Venta must have had between 20,000 and 25,000 inhabitants, including women, children and those too old to work.

The construction of the monumental basalt sculptures placed symmetrically along the length of the sacred center is just as remarkable. Some of them – colossal heads and monolithic altars – weigh over ten tons. Yet the nearest basalt quarries are about 40 miles away, and the volcanic rock employed by Olmec sculptors had to be transported over 80 miles of waterways.

The existence of specialized trades such as stone-cutting, quarrying, sculpting, surveying, etc., implies a highly organized administration. That the Olmecs were an advanced civilization is shown, furthermore, by the fine execution of objects discovered in depositories at La Venta. These consist of highly polished axes, rock crystal beads, jade statuettes, figurines in delicately carved stone, some of which represent crowds watching a ceremony.

Perhaps the most unusual find at La Venta was a group of highly polished concave mirrors, made of hematite, magnetite and ilmenite. They have diameters ranging from 2 to 4 centimeters, with focals varying between 8 and 57 centimeters. They had a specific function in the worship of the sun since they were able to ignite tinder by concentrating the rays of the sun.

Also among the numerous remains were large mosaic paving stones depicting huge stylized heads of jaguars. The jaguar symbolized rain and was considered sacred by pre-Columbians.

The principal pre-Columbian divinities, sun and rain, were already being worshiped at this early period. Despite subsequent differences of names and representations, they were always to form the poles of Indian religion.

Some stone monuments were inscribed with symbols that may have represented numerals. The Olmec system of writing was possibly related to that used later by the Mayans and the inhabitants of Monte Alban.

All of this suggests that the Olmec civilization was the first great manifestation of Indian genius. The art of the builders to whom we owe the remarkable creations of the pre-Columbian world stemmed from La Venta. Indeed the influence of the Olmecs spread from their native coastal regions as far as Tlatilco, on the high plateaux near Mexico City, where statuettes similar to those found in the La Venta depositories have been discovered.

Amerindian architecture was established at La Venta about 1000 B.C. Its typology was to remain unchanged; and it is significant that the two primary types of Middle American constructions – pyramid and ballcourt – are both present at La Venta. The strict plan of the city reflects the hierarchical society which created it; and the plan was to recur in almost all Mexican sacred cities.

We have seen, then, that a civilization with an important ceremonial center existed in the lowlands near the Gulf of Mexico during the 9th century B.C. This is also confirmed by the Olmecs' colossal sculptures which have the megalithic character common to all early great cultures – Egypt, Greece, etc. During this age man discovered the scope of freestone in his artistic interpretation of his beliefs. The results are often marked by a kind of emotional violence – that of a society drunk on its sense of new-found power – and is revealed in the colossal dimensions of both buildings and statuary. This, however, does not apply to Olmec architecture, since their territory was at too great a distance from regions containing the kind of hard stone required for such pyramids and buildings. On the other hand, the Olmecs indulged their passion for the monumental in sculpture: enormous heads, altars, reliefs, basalt pillars. Blocks transported from distant quarries sometimes weighed as much as fifty tons. For a people ignorant of the principals of mechanics and hoists, these are remarkable achievements.

The Olmecs were not alone in their lack of a cyclopean architecture. Even in regions with numerous quarries there are no signs of a megalithic stage of architecture. With the exception, perhaps, of the 'Danzantes' period at Monte Alban, dressed walls cannot be found in Mexico. The impressive stone mounds of Peru and the Nile Valley do not exist in Middle America. The first cultures of the Mexican classical period inherited their use of beaten earth from the Olmecs; and it is not so much the dimensions of the individual parts of the buildings as the overall quantity of material that characterizes the early architecture of the high plateaux. The technological tradition of La Venta was in this way preserved and perpetuated.

Although Tlatilco shows signs of Olmec influence, there were other examples of pre-classical culture in the central Meseta: communities were soon established both on the high plateaux and in the valleys of central Mexico and Oaxaca. Zacatenco, near the Mexican capital, dates from the fourteenth century (as shown by Carbon 14), and sacred cities were built at El Arbolillo, Copilco and Tlapacoya. There was a general awakening throughout Middle America. This pre-classical period, characterized by its achievements in irrigation, agriculture and the manufacture of ceramics, was to culminate in the first great constructions of the high plateaux: the pyramids of Cuicuilco, Cholula and Teotihuacan.

Cuicuilco

Architectural evidence in the central Meseta dates from the 5th century B.C. At Cuicuilco, near the entrance to the present University City of Mexico (built on a lava field), archeologists discovered well-preserved remains beneath several feet of basalt rock. The site was buried when the volcano Xitle erupted in the pre-Christian era, and can in some respects be considered the Herculaneum of Indian America. The remains have enabled archeologists to reconstruct the earliest pre-Columbian architecture on the high plateaux. Although the tough covering layer – 15 to 25 feet thick – had to be dynamited, we can nevertheless trace the development from a simple mound of earth of which early sanctuaries were built to the final impressive pyramid, constructed of huge quantities of material.

The first platform-pyramid seems to owe nothing to La Venta, being circular and not quadrangular in shape. The fragmentary base consists of four superimposed levels. Its dimensions are the best indication of its size: the first level is 445.5 feet in diameter and 25.4 feet high, the second 383 feet in diameter and 16.5 feet high, the third 340 feet in diameter and 11.6 feet high, and the fourth 231 feet in diameter and 10 feet high. The pyramid is over 60 feet high and has a volume of about 3,530,000 cubic feet.

Archeologists examined the monument by means of tunnels bored into its mass. These revealed that it was constructed mainly of beaten earth held in place by large, roughly squared rocks, about 6 feet high by 3.3 feet thick. Deeply embedded and arranged in concentric circles extending to the edge of each platform, the rocks thus prevented the mass of earth from collapsing – because of its weight, some

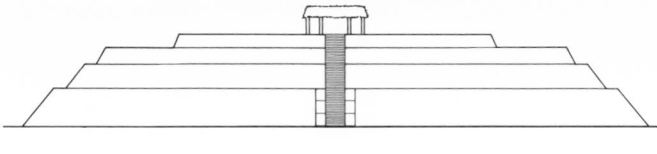

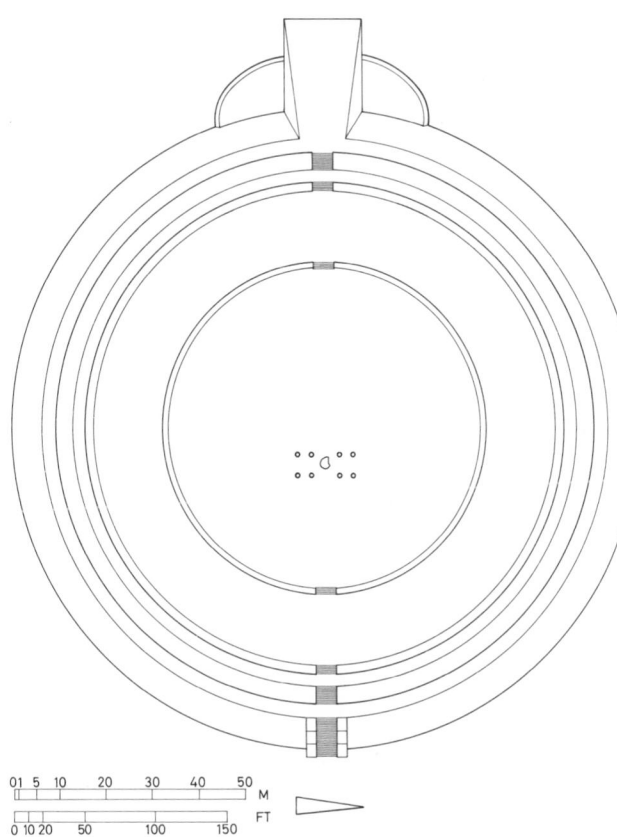

01 5 10   20   30   40   50   M
0 10 20   50   100   150   FT

Elevation and plan of the circular pyramid at Cuicuilco,
near Mexico City

250,000 tons, it would tend to 'flow.' The core of the pyramid is formed of stones cemented by beaten earth. The absence of mortar or limestone is typical of the still very primitive stage of pre-Columbian construction.

Boring also revealed that the pyramid was built in two successive stages. About the 5th or 4th centuries B.C. the platform consisted only of two levels; it was only 42 feet high, although the diameter was the same as in the final version. Later two other levels were added to this base, and were probably completed long before the 3rd or 2nd centuries B.C. when Xitle erupted.

Excavation revealed ramps and staircases on the east and west faces of the mound, and holes for posts or stakes near the center of the top level; this suggests that the pyramid served as a base for a sanctuary. The sanctuary was probably constructed of perishable materials, like the temple at La Venta: wood, thatch and wattle. Although there are only traces of the sanctuary it must have resembled the usual type of Mexican peasant dwelling. The sides of the pyramid were covered with large stone pebbles that perhaps once supported a smooth layer of earth –forerunner of the stucco facings commonly used during the Teotihuacan period.

Cuicuilco was abandoned after the eruption of Xitle. For thousands of years, as indeed even today, Mexico's high plateaux were subject to violent earth tremors; the central Meseta is surrounded by the craters of extinct volcanoes. Usually, the rich volcanic soil attracted settlers who remained until another eruption destroyed their communities. No-one, however, returned to Cuicuilco, and it lay buried for all time beneath layers of barren rock.

None the less, the city left posterity the plan of its circular pyramid; it was to be used up to the time of the Conquest for innumerable monuments dedicated to the gods of the wind. This is another instance of the way in which Mexican architecture was established and perpetuated from its earliest appearance.

Yet another form of construction found at Cuicuilco was to recur throughout pre-Columbian history. This was the stepped pyramid. Like the funerary monuments of Djoser at Saqqara, the first pyramid on the high plateaux consisted of superimposed levels. The monument at La Venta, on the other hand, was formed not of superimposed platforms, but constituted a true pyramid, with even faces and a relatively slight angle which followed the natural slope of the soil. Indeed, until limestone and plaster were employed, the angle remained slight. In this way architects were able to make the construction comparatively stable. (The steepest slopes are found in Mayan regions, where they often exceed 60 degrees for a height of nearly 180 feet; but we must remember that the Mayans used a unique form of cement to manufacture concrete.) However, while constructional methods were based on the use of beaten earth held in place by roughly pointed stone blocks the angle of the apothegm could never exceed 35 to 40 degrees.

The pyramid at Cholula and superimpositions

At Cholula, in the south-eastern state of Puebla, archeologists discovered a huge construction resembling a natural hill, that was found to be almost as old as the pyramid at Cuicuilco. (Remains dating from the Zacatenco-Copilco period, about 1200 B.C., were also found at Cholula.) On its summit is a church built at the time of the Conquest. The pyramid consists of a number of successive superimpositions and additions made from the 2nd century B.C. to the 12th century A.D. The principal constructional period occured during the first century A.D.

Incorporated in the Cholula pyramid is one of the primary pre-Columbian architectural laws: that of superimposition. The pre-Columbians usually enlarged or embellished their pyramid-temples by constructing a new building around the first, the final version being the product of a series of constructions each of which includes the one before. We may compare these buildings to giant onions or nests of tables. The best preserved versions are very often the oldest, for they have been spared the ravages of both time and man.

This feature has provided archeologists with valuable information; it is a form of architectural stratigraphy and so enables us to trace the exact succession of styles and stages of construction. We also know how pre-Columbians built pyramids whose volume equals the greatest Pharaonic achievements.

There is nothing unusual about the re-employment of a sacred place; indeed, it is a characteristic of religions all over the world, and irreconcilable beliefs are often united by common respect for a sacred site. At Byblos (Lebanon) superimpositions have been customary from the fourth millenium up to the present. Starting from neolithic cults, successive religions have been revealed by remains in Egypt, Palestine, among the Amorites, Hyksos, Persians, Greeks and Romans, followed by the early Christians, Byzantines, Arabs and Crusaders. The pre-Columbians followed a similar pattern, and Cholula is but one outstanding example.

The evolution of the pyramid is remarkable: the earliest construction measured 373 feet by 353 feet by 59.4 feet high, with a 6 or 7 degree slope; the final version measures 1155 feet by 1023 feet by 181.5 feet high. The volume is 105,900,000 cubic feet, equivalent to 7 million tons of material. Some six centuries separate the two stages; the first dates from the 2nd century B.C., and employs limestone and stucco – thus suggesting that it was begun after the Cuicuilco pyramid. The three or four superimpositions enclosing the first stage were completed by the time Teotihuacan was destroyed, about the 5th century A.D. Additional remains show that modifications were made up to the 12th century A.D. That worship at the site continued until the Conquest has been attested to by sixteenth-century Spanish observers and historians.

Teotihuacan

Contemporary with the early stages of the Cholula pyramid was the great pyramid of the Sun at Teotihuacan. It marks the first attempt to build a huge monument from scratch (although a small substructure was found in 1960); and it served as the base for a temple which dominated the largest pre-Columbian city of the central Meseta. Twenty-five miles north of Mexico City, this great sacred metropolis played a major role in the development of ancient Mexican civilizations. To some extent, Teotihuacan, the 'City of the Gods,' is the center of the pre-Columbian classical world. Located at a height of 7000 feet, the group of pyramids, esplanades, avenues and palaces – all in ruins when the Conquistadores arrived – was believed by the inhabitants to have been founded by the gods themselves in the mists of time. Sixteenth-century Aztecs knew nothing of the city's founders, nor of the divinities to whom the temples and sanctuaries had been dedicated, although the sites were still venerated.

Names of buildings both in the sacred city and the surrounding town are traditional and perhaps, therefore, incorrect; they were adapted from the Indian by the first white settlers. Nevertheless they must to some extent correspond to the original names. Certain features of the Pyramid of the Sun, for example, suggest that a primordial sun god was worshiped here.

By its dimensions alone the Pyramid of the Sun – the principal monument in the sacred city – indicates how advanced were its creators. It is clearly not a preliminary attempt at something greater, and its antecedents never attained the same dimensions (the final version of the Cholula pyramid was built long after the completion of the Pyramid of the Sun). Its measurements speak for themselves: length of base 742.5 feet; breadth 732.6 feet; surface area, approximately 545,000 square feet. The upper esplanade is 207.9 feet high. More than two and a half million tons of material were used, an overall volume of 35,300,000 cubic feet.

The second most important monument at Teotihuacan is the Pyramid of the Moon. It measures

Section showing the various superimpositions of the great pyramid at Cholula

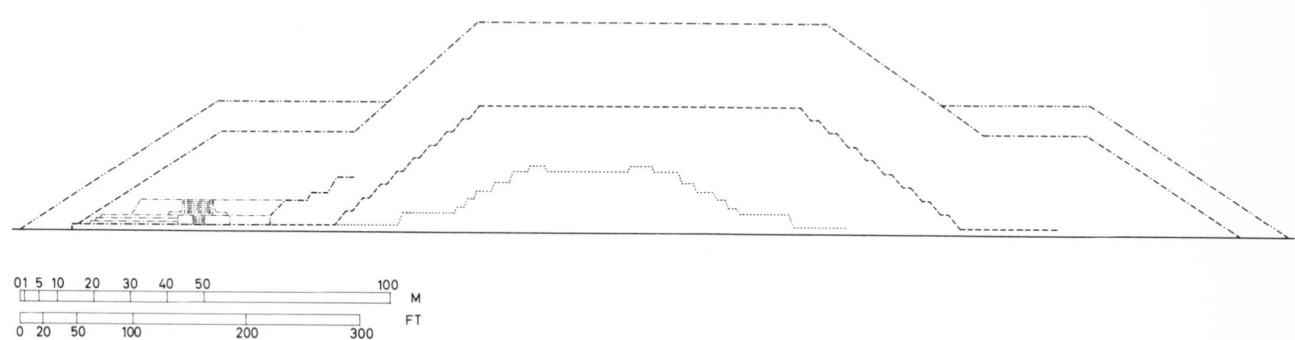

495 feet by 462 feet, with a surface area of approximately 216,000 square feet. It is 138.6 feet high, with a volume of about 12,355,000 cubic feet, and a weight of about 900,000 tons.

The sacred ensemble at Teotihuacan includes a broad axial avenue bordered by various buildings, called the Causeway of the Dead – although it served no funerary purpose and had no connections with the worship of the dead. Opposite the Pyramid of the Moon and with one side bordering the Causeway is the great enclosure surrounding the Temple of Quetzalcoatl, the Plumed Serpent. The enclosure is known as the 'Citadel,' although there is no evidence to suggest it had a military or defensive function. Directly before the Pyramid of the Moon is an open square surrounded by stepped platforms, called the Square or Quadrilateral of the Moon.

The sacred complex covered an area of about 2 square miles. The actual city, however, was considerably larger: including the palaces, it extended over 9 square miles, and at its height of expansion had a surface area of 12.5 square miles. Teotihuacan is probably the finest example of pre-Columbian town planning, not only because of its size but also in the systematic organization and administration that its plan involved.

Excavations

Large-scale excavations at Teotihuacan, which began at the turn of the century, aimed at casting light on the civilization responsible for its creation, and also determining the age of the huge complex. Sixty years ago all the buildings looked like mounds or small hills, overgrown with aloes, branched cacti and shrubs – as is commonly the case in these regions.

The Pyramid of the Sun was restored between 1906 and 1910. Mistakenly, as it later turned out, early archeologists carried out modifications on the structure. Previous experience of pre-Columbian

constructions led them to assume that the ruined pyramid must enclose an earlier version. However, as we now know, their search was in vain for no earlier pyramid existed (apart from the recently discovered minor substructure). By 1939 tunnels bored into the pyramid had definitely proved that it had been built from scratch.

However, the largest pyramid in the Citadel was found to enclose a very interesting earlier construction. This had a series of decorative sculptures on its chief face, flanking either side of a broad axial staircase. The motifs were carved in high and bas-relief and depicted the Plumed Serpent together with geometrically stylized masks of the god of rain, Tlaloc.

Chronology

Some of the early excavations have had debatable results, and reconstructions do not always satisfy present-day requirements. Yet on the whole the work of the first archeologists did succeed in establishing the general outlines of Teotihuacan history. Stratigraphy has made it possible to divide the history into four principal periods, until recently dated between the 3rd and 9th centuries A.D. (see Marquina). However, research by Pina Chan among others has established the dates 400 B.C. to 800 A.D. (see 'Congreso Internacional de Americanistas, Actas y Memorias,' Mexico 1964). According to this theory, Teotihuacan was at its height during the second and third periods, that is, from about 100 A.D. to 600–650 A.D.; the transition from Teotihuacan II to III occurred about 250 A.D. Alfonso Caso and Moreno are among those who clearly show that the end of Teotihuacan III must have occurred in the 7th century.

Yet specialists are once again questioning the validity of these dates following excavations and restoration recently completed in the area of the Pyramid of the Moon by the Mexican government. This extensive and hitherto unprecedented survey of the city began in 1963; fifteen hundred researchers and eight archeologists led by Professor Bernal began a systematic study of the Square of the Moon and neighboring buildings. In eighteen months a group of buildings extending as far as the Causeway of the Dead were almost wholly restored (an area over 1650 feet wide and 1¼ miles long). The size of the operation can be judged by its cost: 18 million pesos, about one and a half million dollars.

The speed with which the undertaking was accomplished obviously provoked criticism – especially of the reconstructions. But, on the whole, the survey was conducted with scientific precision, particularly the research that first identified then restored the palace of Quetzalpapalotl, situated south-west of the Square of the Moon. This building is of major importance: it is the only residence of the classical period that has been fully restored, and it provides valuable information about the life of the priests and dignitaries of Teotihuacan; moreover specialists have been able to determine its age exactly by means of wood and cinder fragments analyzed by Carbon 14.

Before taking a closer look at the architecture of Teotihuacan we must consider the problems of dating raised by this survey. It will undoubtedly affect all pre-Columbian civilizations – indeed, to such an extent that some specialists have been reluctant to draw final conclusions because this would cause numerous earlier theories to be categorically rejected.

New datings

Stratigraphy has revealed that the palace of Quetzalpapalotl dates from the end of Teotihuacan III which, as we have noted, was until recently thought to have occurred about the mid-7th century A.D. The wood-roofed palace, however, together with all the other great Teotihuacan monuments, was set on fire by invading tribes. Their destruction marks the end of the city's most splendid period, although it

existed during a fourth and final period. Mexican archeologists used the Carbon 14 process to obtain the age of the buildings, and results were, to say the least, disconcerting, for they in no way confirmed hitherto generally accepted dates.

We must bear in mind that the wood taken from the palace beams for analysis could not itself give the age of the building, but only the age of the tree of which it had been part. Once the tree had been felled and died its Carbon 14 content began to be discharged by radioactivity. However, it is more than probably that the tree was used soon after it was cut down; builders were unlikely to have used very old wood for so important a construction. They would have left the wood to season for only a few years, to ensure against the possibility of warping.

The ages of most of the wood samples analyzed by the University of California at Los Angeles range between 1750, 1700 and 1730 years, with a margin of about 80 years. This means that the door frames and roof-beams of the palace of Quetzalpapalotl can be dated between 200 and 250 A.D. – the beginning of Teotihuacan III. However, archeologists have subdivided this third period into Teotihuacan III and Teotihuacan IIIA, and according to stratigraphy the palace dates from the latter period. Furthermore, judging by its method of construction the palace is unlikely to have been occupied for more than 150 or 200 years. The heavy masonry roofing rested on a framework of wooden joists 13 to 16 feet long, but the mediocre quality of the stucco and mortar could never have protected the wood from damp during the annual rainy seasons. Built around 250 A.D. the palace must therefore been destroyed about 450 A.D., some two hundred years later. This was also the date when, according to Bernal, the whole city was razed to the ground – not, as was hitherto believed, 650 A.D. Consequently Teotihuacan III began at least two centuries earlier than the most recently proposed dates. The period no longer vacillates between 250 A.D. and 650 A.D., but is now definitely believed to have been from 50 A.D. to 450 A.D.

Once again the Carbon 14 process has been responsible for these radical revisions. Results published in September 1964 by the Instituto Nacional de Antropologia e Historia of Mexico are no longer acceptable. Even Jorge A. Acosta, the author of the report on the findings at the Palace of Quetzalpapalotl, inclines to an earlier chronology based on ceramics, and according to which Teotihuacan III and IIIA should be dated between 250 A.D. and 650 A.D. This attitude is understandable, especially as the latest theories will probably affect a number of pre-Columbian cultures.

Teotihuacan's influence on Kaminaljuyu

The greatest culture of the Mexican classical period, Teotihuacan's influence spread throughout Middle America. Decorative and, above all, ceramic objects of Teotihuacan style are often found at great distances from the city. When ceramics identical to those of the Teotihuacan IIIA period are found 100, 300 and sometimes even 600 miles away from Teotihuacan, the strata in which they are discovered are probably contemporary with this period. The assumption is based on the system of 'indicative' potsherds.

In addition to Teotihuacan-style remains found at Monte Alban, Tajin, and in Mayan regions, archeologists have come across traces of a far more significant connection: the existence of 'colonies' of the City of the Gods. Kaminaljuyu, near Guatemala City, and over 680 miles from Teotihuacan, had apparently been one of these colonies.

The style of Kaminaljuyu buildings clearly derives from Teotihuacan, and, indeed, all the architectural features of the great capital of the high plateaux can be found here. Yet both climate and physical features differ from those of the Central Meseta. Numerous mounds indicate the importance of Kam-

inaljuyu, whose origins go right back to the middle of the pre-classical era, to the 16th century B.C. – the time of the first high plateau cultures at El Arbolillo and Tlatilco. Thus Kaminaljuyu existed long before any influence from the people of Teotihuacan could have made itself felt. Its classic period is nevertheless marked by the appearance of a large number of monuments whose style comes directly from Teotihuacan. What, then, can have happened?

Turning to what is always the most valuable type of archeological evidence – that of ceramic remains – we find that after a certain period, pieces in the style of Teotihuacan become far too numerous to have been merely imported from the city. The Teotihuacan-style ceramics found at Kaminaljuyu were undoubtedly manufactured on the spot. There are two possible explanations for this: conquest or migration. We know, however, that in the pre-Columbian world the making of pottery was always a woman's task, and therefore the possibility of a military conquest and occupation – even of some duration – would not serve to explain the appearance in Guatemala both of a ceramics industry of the type found in Teotihuacan and also of an architecture identical with that of the high plateaux. We must therefore conclude that the soldiers who settled at Kaminaljuyu were accompanied by their womenfolk and families.

What caused a highly civilized community to cross 1000 miles of mountainous country with passes over 12,000 feet high, travel through humid coastal plains and then settle high up in Guatemala – all this at a time when neither wagons nor any form of mounted transport existed?

Trade resulted in the exchange of products over great distances and ideas spread by word of mouth across the whole of pre-Columbian America; there was therefore no apparent need for long-established communities to revert to a nomadic state. Migration

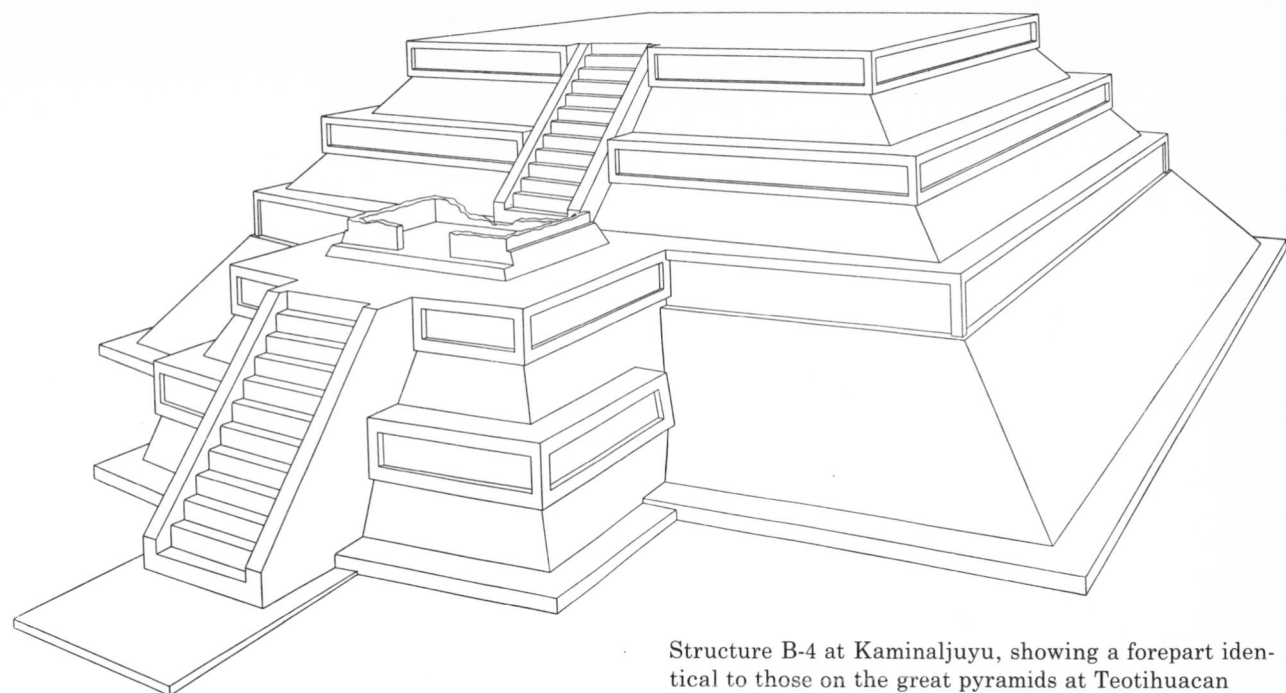

Structure B-4 at Kaminaljuyu, showing a forepart identical to those on the great pyramids at Teotihuacan

could only have been motivated by invasion, or attempts to throw off the yoke of the conqueror.

Alfred Ridder, Jesse Jennings and Edwin Shook, who instigated excavations at Kaminaljuyu, put forward this theory in a report published by the Carnegie Institution of Washington: 'There is evidence, from archeological remains, of movements of population rather than simple cultural influences.' The age of the layer (known as 'Esperanza') in which Teotihuacan-style monuments were discovered has been almost exactly determined by correlating it with neighboring Mayan chronology. The layer is also contemporary with the Monte Alban III period and Tajin. The resulting network, based on the discoveries made in the one layer, enables us to trace the succession of events.

Long-established connections, dating perhaps from the second century, existed between Teotihuacan, Kaminaljuyu, numerous Peruvian cities, and western Guatemala. The rout and destruction of Teotihuacan occurred about 450 A.D. and the survivors fled south. But neighboring territories were either hostile or already occupied by the invaders, and so the Teotihuacans were forced to continue their march. They finally halted at Kaminaljuyu – where, assured of their welcome, they founded a 'New Teotihuacan.' Here they were to reestablish their beliefs, traditions, and art. Kaminaljuyu became a replica of Teotihuacan, a paler version perhaps, but none the less of great significance.

Kaminaljuyu-Teotihuacan dates, then, from 450 A.D. or 500 A.D., and these dates coincide both with Mayan and other historical events, in so far as archeologists have been able to reconstruct them.

The invasions

Which tribes were responsible for the downfall of the greatest central Mexican civilization? In order to understand the sequence of events that led to the destruction of Teotihuacan (the site was finally abandoned two centuries later), we must refer to a parallel case: the migration of the Toltecs, which resulted in the reconstruction of Chichen-Itza in central Yucatan.

Towards the end of the 10th century A.D., tribes from the city of Tula, some sixty miles north of Mexico City, began moving south-east. They eventually settled some 700 miles away from their starting-point, at Chichen-Itza, an ancient Mayan city which they soon transformed. Situated north of the Yucatan peninsula on flat coastal land, the new Mayan-Toltec city was to bring about a remarkable 'renaissance' of the Mayan world.

The transformation of Kaminaljuyu followed a

Structure A-7 at Kaminaljuyu, showing the characteristic mounds and panels of Teotihuacan. The upper sanctuary was thatched, like the huts of all pre-Columbian Indians

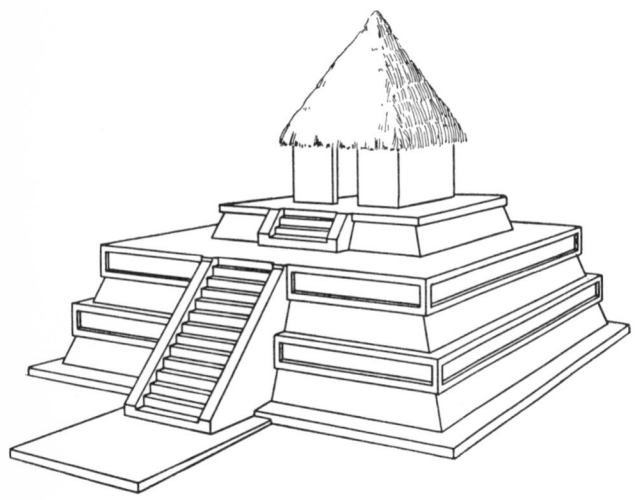

similar pattern – with one significant difference: while Kaminaljuyu always remained a 'copy' of Teotihuacan – important, certainly, since there are no less than 200 pyramids in an area of 20 square miles – Chichen-Itza marks the pinnacle of Toltec architecture. Using the false masonry vault (that unique invention inherited from the Mayans), the Toltecs of Chichen-Itza made their capital a 'super-Tula.' The migrations are an intriguing subject: five centuries before the Toltecs an equally great civilization left its native regions high in the central Meseta to settle 600 miles south in alien territory – alien in fauna, flora and in climate.

Assuming that similar causes lead to similar results we have to conclude that in both cases migration followed invasion by nomadic tribes from the north. This also occurred in Europe, where communities on the Mediterranean coasts were regularly invaded and destroyed: waves of Achaeans, Dorians, Celts and Gauls, Vandals, Visigoths, Franks, Avars, Goths, Alamans and Huns ravaged these shores. The nomads that swept down from the plains of North America resemble the barbarian hordes who came from Germany, Russia and Siberia. The pattern is the same: periods of stability, when the nomads' advance could be checked, alternated with unsettled times when all was reduced to chaos and confusion.

The movements of population increased. In the Old World the impetus originated in the central Asian steppes. Driven by famine and drought, tribes left their native regions to plunder the accumulated possessions of settled communities. Widespread warfare followed; its ebb and flow was to affect both the Romans and the kingdoms that succeeded them, and both ultimately succumbed to the barbarians' repeated assaults.

The invasions of Middle America also occurred at fairly regular intervals: fall of Teotihuacan, 450 A.D.; final destruction of Teotihuacan, probably by the Toltecs who founded Tula, 650 A.D.;

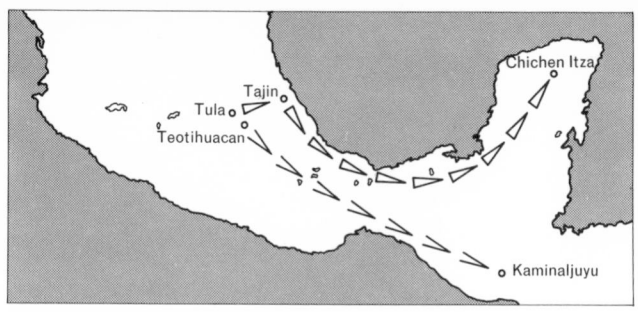

Map showing the great migrations. In the 5th century groups of Teotihuacans left their destroyed city to settle in Kaminaljuyu. In the 10th century Toltecs left Tula, passed through Tajin and settled in Chichen Itza

950 A.D., first attack on Tula by the Chichimecs, resulting in the migration of a Toltec ruler to Chichen-Itza; Tula existed until the 12th century A.D.; in 1168 A.D., Tula falls to the Chichimecs, now sufficiently powerful to consolidate their conquests; about 1250 A.D. the Chichimecs, now established at Tenayuca, were conquered by the Aztecs, newcomers to the pre-Columbian scene; they were to dominate almost all of Middle America until the arrival of the Conquistadores.

This sequence of events clearly demonstrates the interdependence of pre-Columbian peoples; it also reveals how adaptable they were to widely differing climates, since they seem to have been equally at home on the high plateaux and in the tropical regions of the lowlands. Because of these movements of population the fundamental unity of ancient Mexican culture was preserved, and its common background constantly renewed, reminding us of the homogeneity of the pre-classical period. The divisions that every great civilization attempts to create are invariably thwarted by migrating tribes. For this reason, no Mexican civilization can be considered a separate entity. Isolationism is not a feature of the Indian world. Indeed, pre-Columbian cultures can only be understood in the light of their interconnections and inter-relationships.

Mountainous regions do not so much separate as unite peoples. Parallels exist between the paintings of Teotihuacan III and the bas-reliefs at Tajin that can only be explained by the existence of continued contacts. What is known about the migrations undoubtedly helps us to understand the part played by trade and the exchange of ideas during settled periods, and also explains why we have to compare very different cultures in order to grasp the significance of certain buildings. Above all, the migrations show to what extent new chronological theories compel radical re-evaluations of numerous civilizations. Assuming Teotihuacan III to be 200 or 250 years older than formerly believed, then similar dates must be applied, for example, to Tajin: pre-Columbians did not develop and expand 'in an island,' removed from all influences and independent of all neighbors.

In addition to tracing the beginnings of architecture in pre-Columbian Middle America, we have tried in this chapter to determine the outlines of a complex history, its migrations, inter-relationships, and the strange laws which were common to all Mexican civilizations. From their first efforts at La Venta in the 9th century B.C. to the Aztecs' concluding period, we have seen that the Mexican Indians were constantly exposed to alternate periods of war and peace. The nomads acted as a kind of piston on the northern frontiers: sometimes their advance was checked but sometimes they were victorious. Then they, in turn, settled in and defended the communities they had seized, while the previous occupiers fled south. The process was repeated when a fresh wave of nomads swept down from the north. The invaders were usually better fighters than the settlers: we know that early German tribes, for example, possessed finer steel than the Romans; and it was the Chichimecs who introduced bow-and-arrow warfare to Mexico.

In the New World, this phenomenon recurred with almost mathematical regularity every two or three centuries. Only a few centers survived assault over long periods, and they were to be the pivots of the pre-Columbian world: Teotihuacan, in existence from 500 B.C. to 450 or 650 A.D.; Monte Alban, for almost a thousand years; Tajin, 2nd century B.C. to 13th century A.D.; and, finally, the Mayans, 2nd century B.C. to the 12th century A.D., with their astonishing powers of recovery and, indeed, of integration. Because of their relative stability, these Mexican regions – the central Meseta, Oaxaca, the Gulf of Mexico and Yucatan – gave to advanced civilizations, an architecture which, despite local variations, is fundamentally similar.

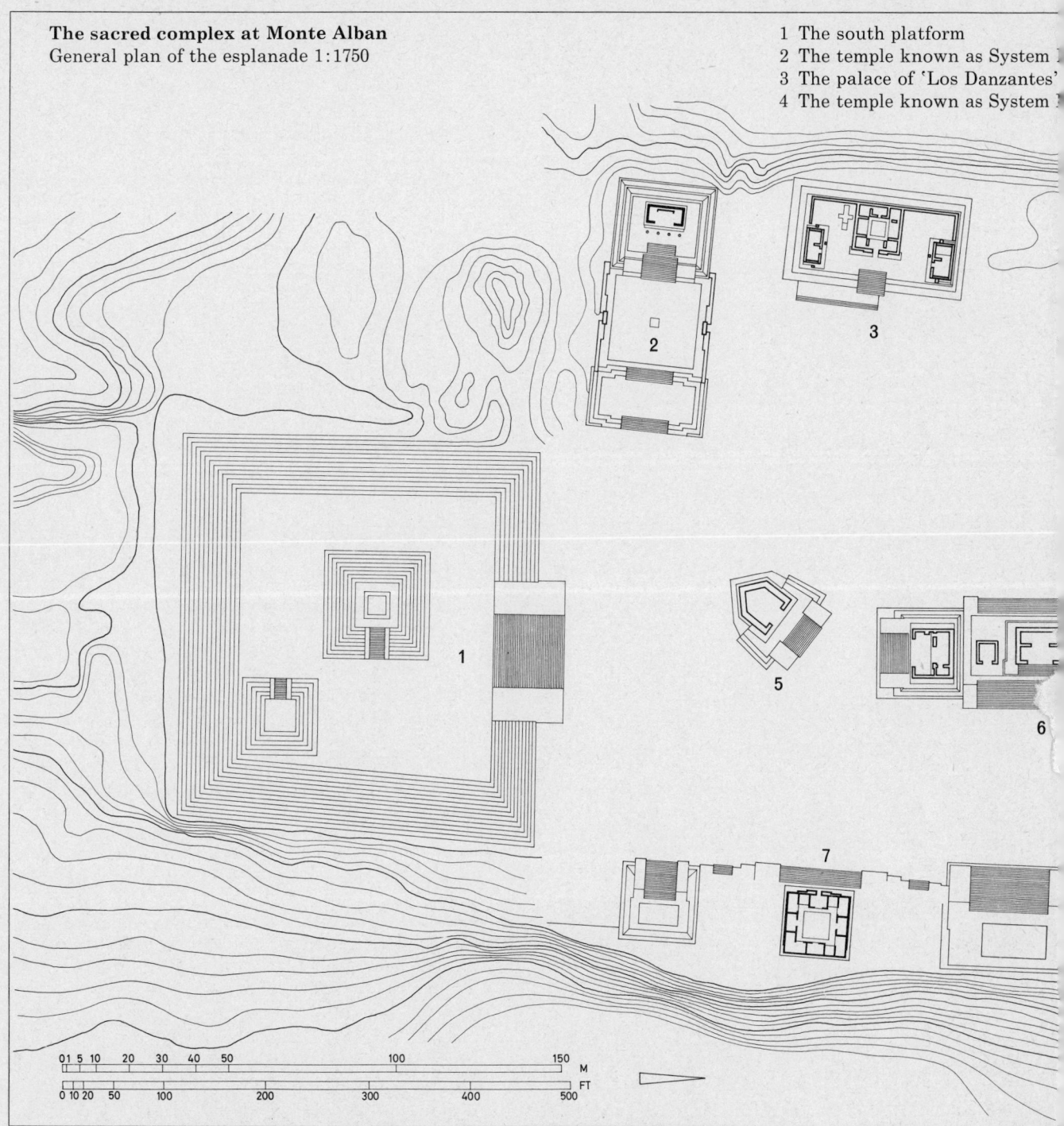

The sacred complex at Monte Alban
General plan of the esplanade 1:1750

1 The south platform
2 The temple known as System
3 The palace of 'Los Danzantes'
4 The temple known as System

01 5 10 20 30 40 50 100 150 M
0 10 20 50 100 200 300 400 500 FT

Notes

Monte Alban and the treasures in the tombs

The sacred capital of the Zapotecs, in the State of Oaxaca, is probably, from an archeological viewpoint, the richest in ancient Mexico. In addition to the numerous monuments that have come to light or that have still to be excavated, the hill of Monte Alban is literally stuffed with tombs cut out of the earth and covered with large blocks of stone.

Some of the 174 tombs discovered to date have extremely rich furnishings. Especially interesting are the ceramics, decorated with motifs in relief. The lintel of the tomb is often surmounted by a niche containing a ceramic funerary urn, depicting a Zapotec divinity. These pieces are among the most valuable sources of information about the pantheon of Monte Alban. Their existence at the tombs' entrances enable us to interpret their meaning: they ensured that the dead person within was protected by a particular god.

Many of the tombs also have polychrome ornamentation. Some – like tombs 104 and 105 – have walls entirely covered with frescoes, in red, blue, yellow, black and white, depicting divinities and priests in processions. The style of these frescoes is related both to works discovered at Teotihuacan (the human figures) and to the reliefs of Tajin (the borders with volutes).

Among the objects found in some of the well-preserved tombs – notably in tomb 7 discovered by Caso – especial mention must be made of the metalwork and jewelry. The most spectacular pre-Columbian treasures were unearthed in this tomb, and today they are the prized possessions of the Museum at Oaxaca.

The execution of the jewels indicates remarkable technical skill; yet on examining them closer, authorities were surprised to find that they were not in fact Zapotec but Mixtec in origin. For a long time they wondered why a Mixtec dignitary had been buried in Monte Alban and not in his own capital, Mitla. Why, too, had such a rich and powerful man been interred in an ancient tomb that had not been constructed for him, but merely emptied of its earlier occupant? Furthermore the tomb, discovered in 1931, was filled with fabulous treasures. Similar cases have provided a satisfactory explanation: long after its decline, Monte Alban continued to be venerated as a sacred city by the inhabitants of surrounding regions – to some extent it was the Rome of the Central Mexican peoples. It was therefore considered an honor to be buried here; and the Mexican ruler thus showed he was descended from Zapotec lineage, with which he probably did have some connection – rather like European emperors in the late Middle Ages who laid claim to the Roman imperial purple.

Yagul and Zaachila

Discoveries made between 1960 and 1962 at Yagul clearly indicate the specialized place of this site, influenced both by the Zapotecs of Monte Alban and the Mixtecs of Mitla. When the former began to decline, and even before the latter reached their height, Yagul served as an intermediary or 'relay post.' The city reached its apotheosis in a transitional period, beginning with Monte Alban IV (about 800 A.D.). However, remains brought to light by Bernal show that the site had been inhabited for a considerable time, since remains dating from Monte Alban I (beginning of 1000 B.C.) were discovered. A number of fine tombs of the Mixtec period were excavated at Yagul. Their furnishings resemble those Caso found at Monte Alban.

At Zaachila, another Mixtec capital, a funerary chamber was discovered to contain jewels and various finely executed ornaments. Most striking, however, is the unusual decoration of the hypogeum; its strong reliefs carved from stone embedded in mortar – and depicting divinities resembling those of the Monte Alban frescoes – seem clearly to forecast the mosaic techniques of Mitla. Yagul has relief decorations, with key-patterns, lozenges and meanders, that forecast, too, the geometric character of the 'White Palaces' of Mitla, which were a technological apotheosis in pre-Columbian Mexico.

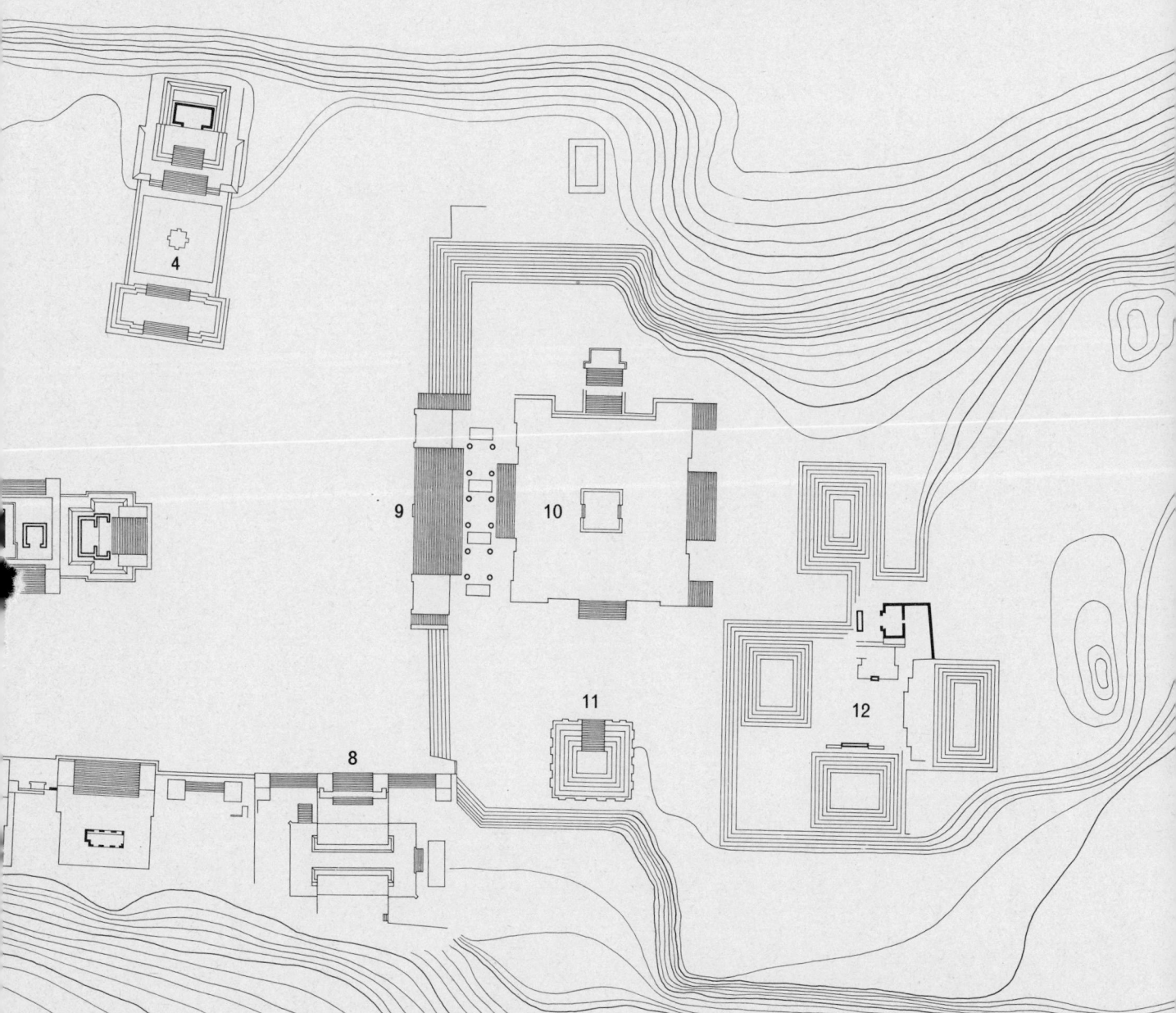

Plates

Monte Alban (Oaxaca)

67 Aerial view of the esplanade at Monte Alban, sacred capital of the Zapotecs, with its pyramids, palaces, observatory and ballcourt.

68 Perspective of the staircase lining the east side of the ceremonial complex that surmounts the esplanade.

69 The sacred complex seen from the north. In the foreground, the northern quadrilateral, with its central altar. At the summit of the staircases, the remains of huge columns that once formed the triumphal portico.

70 The great northern staircase, 132 feet wide. In the foreground, a stele decorated in bas-relief.

71 The temple called System IV. The structure of this building is similar to that of temple M: a quadrilateral before a pyramid.

72 The pyramid of System IV. It is surmounted by a sanctuary of which only the base of the walls and columns remain today.

73 Detail of a typical Monte Alban cornice, at the summit of temple IV. The shewback border stresses the summit of the wall, above the inclined plane that precedes a vertically placed projection, itself bordered by an overhanging frieze.

74 The esplanade at Monte Alban seen from the summit of the south staircase. In the foreground, the Observatory.

75 The Observatory staircase, bordered by broad walls.

76 Front view of the Observatory. At right: the opening of the arched passage that runs through the building.

77 The arched passage of the Observatory. In the background, the south staircase of the esplanade.

78 The ballcourt at Monte Alban. Detail of the lateral staircase and inclined plane, bordered by a stepped embankment typical of Zapotec ballcourts.

79 Axial view of the ballcourt, taken from the summit of the northern staircase. The small projections on the sloping lateral planes supported the thick layer of stucco that once covered the whole monument.

80 Three of the Monte Alban 'Danzantes.' These archaic sculptures are related to certain Olmec bas-reliefs, and also reveal the earliest form of hieroglyphics – which has still not been deciphered.

81 Megalithic vaulting in a tomb at Monte Alban: enormous blocks are propped together in pairs.

Yagul (Oaxaca)

82 Ballcourt recently excavated by Professor Ignacio Bernal. An example of restoration.

83 The priests' quarters, with palaces whose patios were surrounded by porticoed galleries.

Mitla (Oaxaca)

84 The palace of Columns, with its geometrical mosaic motifs: key-patterns, meanders, lozenges, etc.

85 The south-west corner of the palace of Columns: the Mixtec element stands out from other pre-Columbian architectural creations because of its precision.

86 Detail of the façade of the palace of Columns, with the subtly placed mosaics that result in a play of light and shadow.

87 The great hall of columns lends its name to the grandest of the Mitla palaces; the six monolithic shafts of volcanic stone are slightly conical in shape.

88 Interior corner of the patio situated behind the hall of columns. The ornamentation is articulated in strongly contrasting rhythms.

89 The patio of the palace of Columns: each of the four rooms surrounding the patio has only one axial doorway.

90 The interior of one of the rooms facing onto the patio of the palace of Columns. It is very dark. The roofing has been hastily restored.

◀ Plans

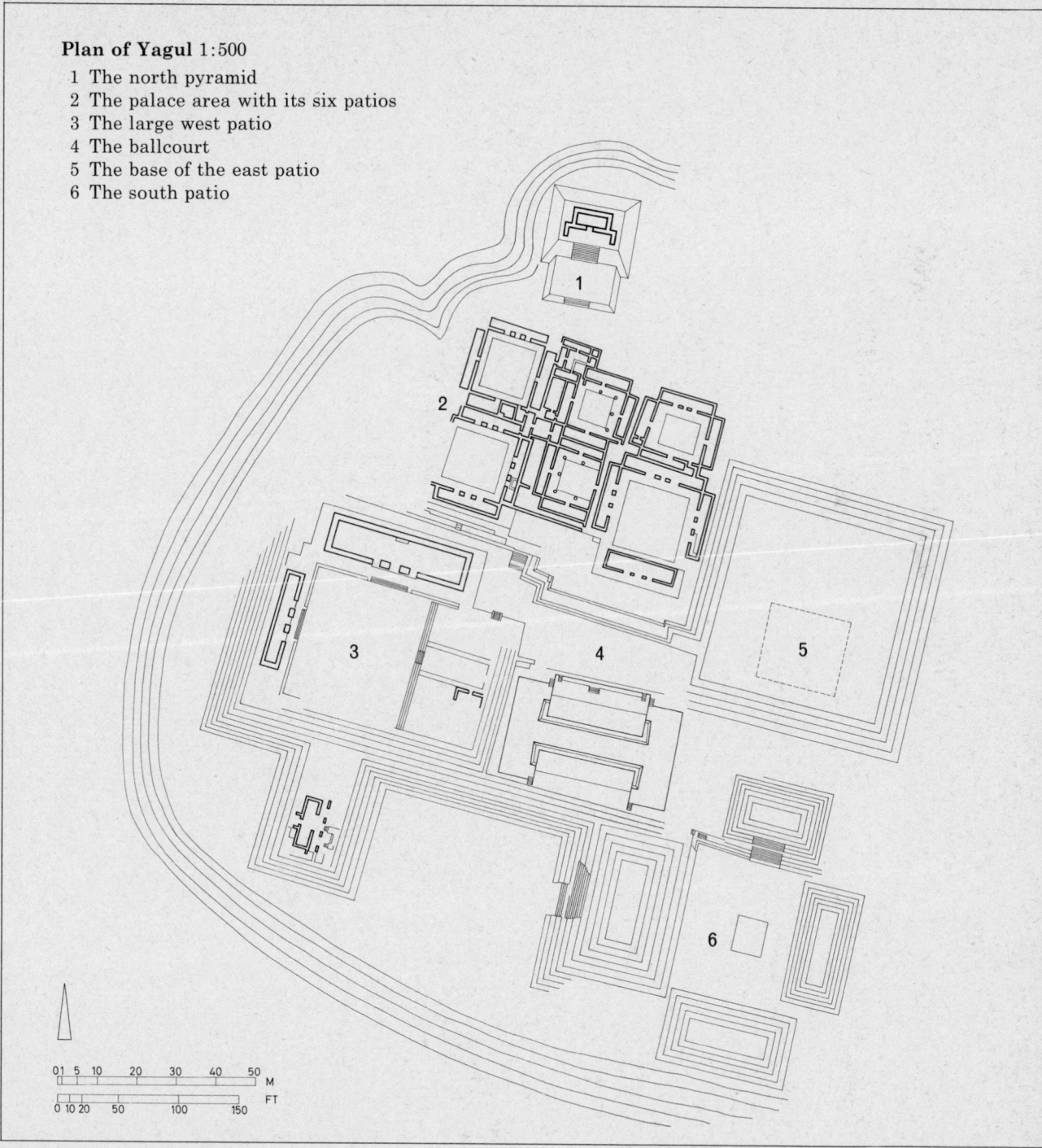

Plan of Yagul 1:500

1 The north pyramid
2 The palace area with its six patios
3 The large west patio
4 The ballcourt
5 The base of the east patio
6 The south patio

0.1 5 10 20 30 40 50 M
0 10 20 50 100 150 FT

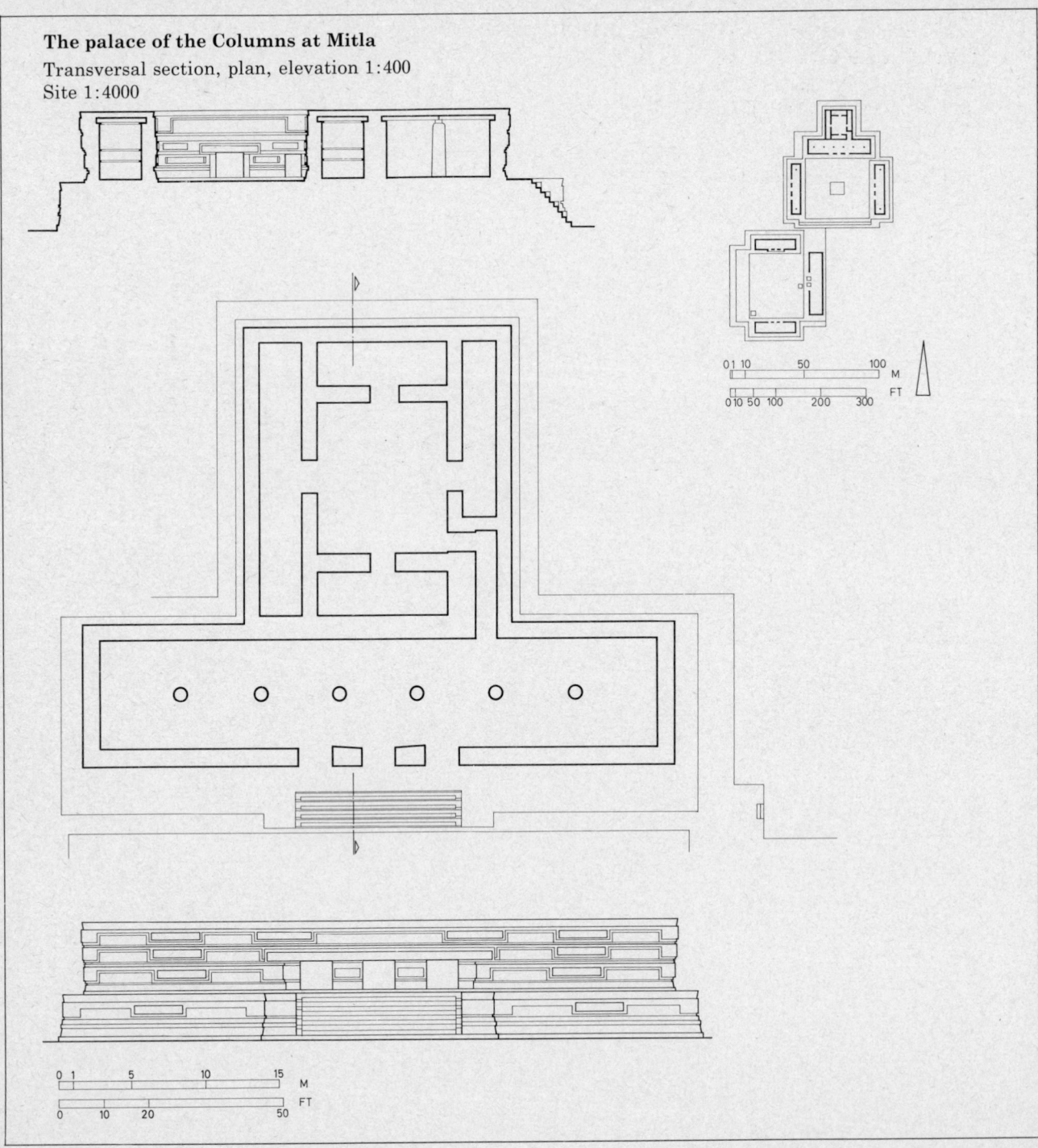

The palace of the Columns at Mitla

Transversal section, plan, elevation 1:400
Site 1:4000

0 1 10   50   100   M

0 10 50 100   200   300   FT

0 1   5   10   15   M

0   10   20   50   FT

3. The Birth of a capital: Teotihuacan

Teotihuacan is located in the center of a vast plain surrounded by extinct volcanoes; and the size and shape of its two great pyramids seem to echo the black conical peaks. Fifty years ago the resemblance was even more marked, for the ruined site was still overgrown with vegetation that for centuries had buried the once sacred city. Today the shapeless mounds have given way to carefully restored perspectives, a play of masses all articulated on the same constructive principle, which creates a kind of rhythmic repetition. We must analyze this fundamental and omnipresent architectonic element before going on to consider the buildings and complexes, because it has to be clearly understood in order to evaluate Teotihuacan's powerfully structured world.

A constant: the panel

The city's esplanades, platforms, pyramids and quadrilaterals all reveal the same plastic rhythm, the same module in the play of volumes, and the same profile of cornices, which are, in fact, more than mere decoration: they form an integral part of a constructional technique peculiar to Teotihuacan. Mexican archeologists call this feature a 'tablero,' and it is best translated by the word 'panel.' Teotihuacan architecture is characterized by the repetition of the long horizontals formed by these panels and their projecting framework. Their construction is based on a very subtle use of the simplest plastic elements: the panel, whose framework consists of a square molding, is not supported by a wall but by an embankment with a 45 to 50 degree slope, which approximates the natural incline of the material.

The panel, with its stepped tiers, is to be found everywhere, facing platforms, temples and esplanades. The core of each building consists of beaten earth and lava stone around which was applied the layer of masonry arranged in superimposed panels (the layer also served as a support for the core). The method of construction was simple and unchanging:

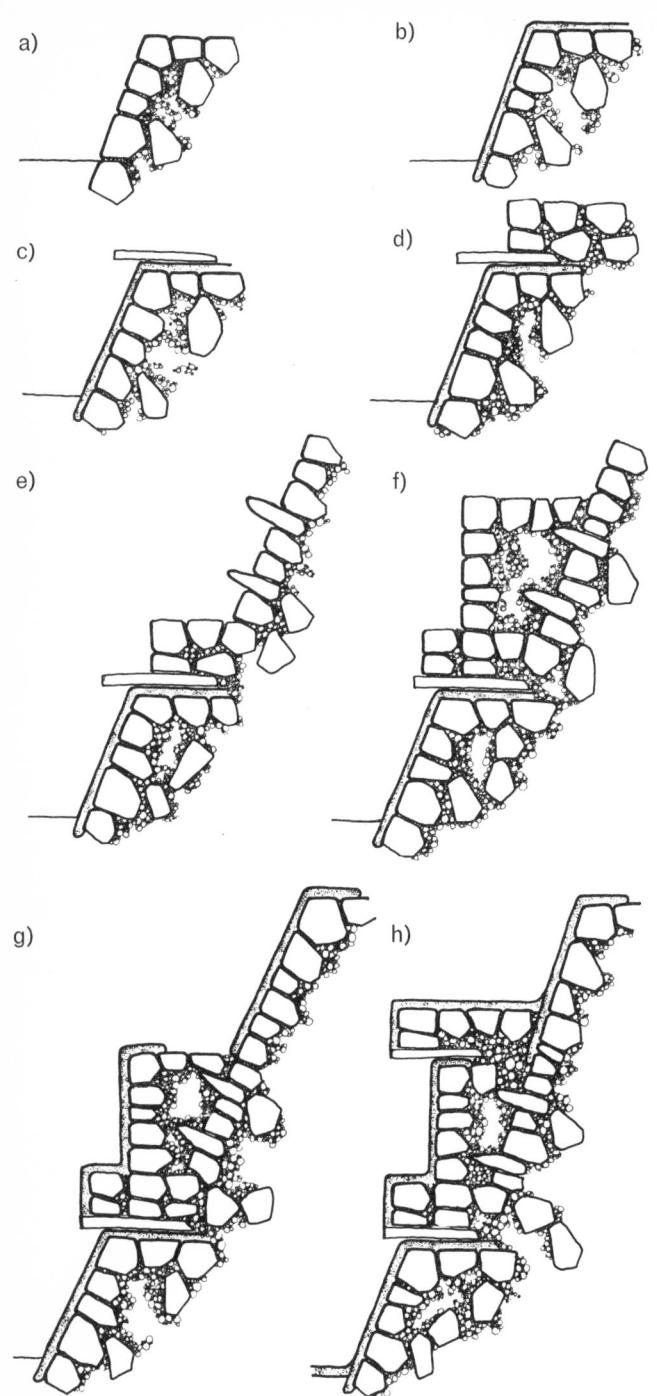

it was based on the use of mortar and limestone which together cemented locally quarried blocks. Roughly shaped, these blocks were usually porous but hard lava stone, red or black in color.

On a 45 degree slope, that seldom exceeded a quarter or half of the total height of the panel, a course of flat stones were erected. These projected over the embankment, their purpose being to support the lower molding of the framework. Once set in place, receding from the border, the panel was surmounted by another projecting course which would form the support for the upper molding. In this way the masonry panel was completely enclosed in a frame in relief.

Only one aesthetic reason governed this system: it consisted of counteracting the fragility of the material, for limestone mortar did not permit the construction of retaining walls. Vertical masonry-work had therefore to be replaced by a stepped order that, to the eye, has neither the gentle lines nor the indeterminate character of volumes created by inclined planes. A uniform surface gives way to a powerful structure, formed of superimposed moldings, each receding from the next; indeed these are of great significance in the construction. Because of their plastic treatment the receding levels throw strong shadows which create rhythm in the volumes and conceal the natural slope of the materials (due to the lack of durable cement builders dared not exceed the natural angle). With the panels spaced out in tiers it was possible to articulate volumes with a remarkable propensity of catching light,

The various stages of the construction of a 'tablero', or panel, characteristic of Teotihuacan architecture unlike smoothly inclined surfaces which are flattened by the direct light of the Tropics.

The panel system clearly had many advantages: the shelving base allowed height with no loss of impact; the fillet of the framework together with the panel – although vertical – never formed a solid mass. The endless possibilities of the system seem, above all, to have fascinated Teotihuacan builders. Indeed, numerous superimpositions could be made, the elements could be elongated without limit, or else arranged in skewbacks. The number of combinations employed is astonishing. Forms progress from the simple platform of square plan with staircases set on one or more sides; then come all the variations made possible by superimposition – small pyramids formed of two, three or four stepped levels, larger monuments with five levels (forerunner of the Pyramid of the Moon) or even six levels (the Temple of Quetzalcoatl in the Citadel). Sometimes the solutions are ingenious: one side of a platform may consist of three levels while the other has only one, set against a terreplein in which the back part of the platform is embedded (the Citadel enclosure). In every case the Teotihuacan panel helped to create volumes that were both pleasing and uniform; and every solution resulted in strong reliefs, with angles stressed by the horizontal and vertical fillets of the framework. The play of light and shadow, and of right-angles, together with the regular succession of levels, are all perfect means of expressing a powerful architecture stemming from a theocratic society.

The standardized structure used by Teotihuacan builders resembles a Meccano set. The most complicated combinations could be achieved from the one fundamental architectural principle. However, there is a stage between plastic discipline and the monotony resulting from total uniformity; and in fact numerous variations existed, in the height of an embankment and a panel, in the width of the framework, in the proportion of the panel to its embankment, or in the length-height relation between the panels themselves. But identical architectonic elements always characterized platforms, quadrilaterals, patios and avenues.

Two primary laws govern – almost tyrannically – the arrangement of the panels. The first is orthogonal, that is, the exact arrangement of component parts according to a right-angled system; and in this respect the right angle governs the vertical position and the frame of the panel as much as the plan, since all the buildings are orientated on the same axes. We shall find that this is so when we consider the plan of Teotihuacan.

The second law is that of symmetry, often a corollary to the first. Individual buildings as well as complexes were subject to strict axial symmetry. However – and this is an important element in the plan of the city – symmetry is respected on only one axis. Orthogonal symmetry rarely occurs (two axes intersecting one another at right angles) although examples can be found in other cultures (such as the pyramid of the Castillo at Chichen-Itza, with its four staircases. Moreover, this applies only to elements that are part of the city, and not to the general outlines. This partly accounts for the marked dynamic quality of Teotihuacan forms.

We must, in conclusion, stress both the functional and plastic contribution made by the staircases. Their monumental flights, bordered by ramps, sometimes interrupted by projections which seem to accent the regular surfaces and so enliven the ascending rhythm, create perspectives that either unite different parallel accesses, or contrast diverging movements. Here, too, the variety of solutions leads to a rich formal vocabulary: some staircases are narrow in proportion to their height, while others are majestically broad, accommodating more than ten people abreast. The former accentuate the ascending movement, and the latter stress the great horizontal lines of the complexes.

Before turning to the individual buildings we must

mention that although the staircases and panels are today covered with a dull and dark layer of lava stone, they were originally painted in bright colors. A thick layer of mortar (6 to 10 cms thick was applied to the masonry framework, followed by a layer of limestone or stucco; frescoes were then painted on this surface. The great city of the high plateaux was not the austere stone city we see today – although it does emphasize its sobriety and economy of means; its sunbathed surfaces, brilliantly colored in red and green, dazzled the eye, and the effect was heightened by walls that had been polished with pumice-stone.

The two great pyramids

The only exceptions to the panel system at Teotihuacan occurred in the pyramids of the Sun and the Moon. They were almost square in plan (the pyramid of the Sun was 742.5 feet by 732.6 feet, the pyramid of the Moon was 495 feet by 462 feet); we have already given their colossal measurements. However, the total amount of material used in the pyramid of the Sun is almost three times as great as that of the pyramid of the Moon, thus indicating the difference in their importance, although their basic form was identical: three superimposed levels, with trapezoidal faces, are separated from the fourth by a vertical projection which counteracts the inclined surfaces forming the mass of both pyramids. This intermediary vertical motif is therefore of great significance. Today it has lost some of its impact for erosion has caused it to sink; and restoration work carried out at the turn of the century did not take this into account. What purpose did the projection serve? Was it merely a plastic element, or did it have a symbolical function in that it stressed the uppermost level which gave access to the 'holy of holies'?

Today the sanctuary which was built on the summit of the pyramid no longer exists, but wall foundations and other remains, together with stone and terracotta models found in the course of excavation, enable us to visualize its original appearance. We must remember that sanctuaries were built not only on the summits of major pyramids but also on the numerous platforms scattered over the sacred city. They consisted of a single room, a 'holy of holies,' which only priests were allowed to enter. Square or rectangular in plan, with one entrance framed in a façade (sometimes divided into three by pillars), the sanctuary was roughly roofed with beams embedded in mortar. Models reveal that it was crowned by a paneled frieze and crenellated ornamentation.

We can thus picture the great pre-Columbian pyramids in their totality. Unfortunately none of the sanctuaries of the early period, particularly at Teotihuacan, have survived, and only now and then can we trace an outline. We know from this, however, that the sanctuary was often divided into two parts, consisting of a vestibule or entrance chamber which gave access to the 'holy of holies.'

The monumental staircases that lead to the temple at the summit of the pyramid of the Sun are very interesting: at the base they consisted of two flights situated on either side of the section projecting from the pyramid's face. The two flights then joined to scale the second level. At the third level they separated again into two parallel flights, and came together to scale the vertical projection and the fourth level.

An altar was probably erected on the front section, in the center of the principal face. The three levels of this forepart – which has been badly restored – were constructed according to the usual Teotihuacan panel system. The section seems to have been added after the completion of the pyramid, and this accounts for the difference in orientation of the forepart in relation of the pyramid; it also accounts for the staircases, awkwardly placed in the angle formed by the face of the pyramid and the forepart. Perhaps the builders were aware that the oblique direction of the staircases was unsatisfactory, for, when they constructed the pyramid of the Moon they adopted a more straightforward solution, placing the staircases on the axis of the building so that they pass over the forepart. The single flight emphasizes the ascending movement of the pyramid. In fact, the solution practically suggested itself, because of the axial arrangement of the Square of the Moon which formed the northern end of the Causeway of the Dead.

If the pyramid of the Sun was dedicated to a solar cult, and if – as we shall show – its orientation was based on the setting sun during the period of its zenithal course, then yet another theory is possible: the two staircases would have played a symbolical role in the worship of the sun. Officiating priests followed the course of the sun as it moved from south to north or from north to south, by climbing the south staircase and descending by the north flight, according to the dates set for ceremonies.

Early borings into the pyramid of the Sun, together with the tunnel bored in 1960 which revealed the existence of a small primitive substructure, have provided valuable information about the method of construction. Enclosing a core formed of a horizontal, compressed layer of beaten earth (which, as the builders knew, might easily be washed away by the seasonal rains) was a layer of stone cemented with mortar, whose purpose was to prevent water seeping in and thus threatening whole structure. Because of its weight the building had a tendency to 'flow', so perpendicular buttresses were added to the sides and embedded in the mass. These supports can be seen today, as a result of the unfortunate attempts made by Batres to 'peel' the outer layer in the hopes of finding a perfectly preserved substructure.

The vast quantity of material – two and a half million tons of stone and earth – constituting the pyramid of the Sun intrigues archeologists – and with good reason: how could a people ignorant of the wheel and lacking beasts of burden or any form of mounted transport construct such a colossal monument?

An agrarian society such as Teotihuacan always had a slack season; all depended on the land and on reserves accumulated by the ruling priests, one of whose tasks was to redistribute supplies as needed. The slack period occurred during the annual four months' drought, and it was then that collective activity was transferred to building the sacred monuments. The priests wished to obtain the favor of the gods of fertility and so directed all efforts towards constructing temples, altars and sanctuaries. This is why the great pyramids and monuments of Teotihuacan came to be built.

If we assume that 3000 laborers participated in the communal undertaking (food was provided) how long would it have taken to complete the pyramid of the Sun? Material had to be transported from increasingly great distances as the land was progressively stripped; the average distance traveled was about two miles. Carrying a load of some 80 lbs a laborer would therefore walk for some two hours, which means that only five journeys could be made each day and the maximum load transported would be 450 lbs.

Some of the laborers would also have been employed in the actual construction. We can therefore assume that 2000 men carried about 400 tons of material a day; and since they worked for only four months of the year, some 50,000 tons were transported in this short period. Estimating that a further 25,000 tons were quarried during the remainder of the year, it follows that the annual amount was 75,000 tons. We know that the pyramid of the Sun is made up of two and a half million tons of stone and earth which means that it took thirty years to build. The pyramid of the Moon was built in about twelve years.

The Square of the Moon

Although the two great pyramids are the most spectacular buildings in Teotihuacan – partly because of their size – there are other constructions which, while smaller, demanded more specialized workmanship. The pyramids required innumerable teams of laborers, but the esplanades and platforms constructed on the panel system called for the skilled services of masons and other specialists.

By its concept of unity, the Square of the Moon, situated before the pyramid of the same name, shows clearly that the Teotihuacan builders knew how to take full advantage of the panel system. The Square is surrounded by twelve platforms of four levels each, and covers an area of about 7.5 acres. There is evidence of repairs and remodeling which, however, did not affect the overall unity. There is a sense of severity, but not aridity, about this Square which indicates a remarkable plastic awareness.

A straightforward study of the plan, as recently reconstructed by Professor Bernal, shows that the arrangement of the buildings cannot have resulted from a single project. A brief analysis will help to explain this: it seems that platforms 2 and 3, together with 4 and 5, which are placed slightly to the rear, were built during a first period, before the construction of the forepart of the Pyramid of the Moon – at least in its present form. The earliest form of the Square must have consisted of two platforms on either side of the Square, in line with the horizontal faces of the Pyramid. When the forepart was added to, the builders decided to construct two more platforms, A and B; to some extent these overshadowed platforms 2 and 3. In order to complete the quadrilateral, platforms C and D and E and F were built. They are not, however, in line with platforms 2 and 3 and 4 and 5. Furthermore, the irregular spaces between C and 2, and C and 4 (and, therefore, D and 3 and D and 5) can only result from the presence of A and B. Clearly, then, the

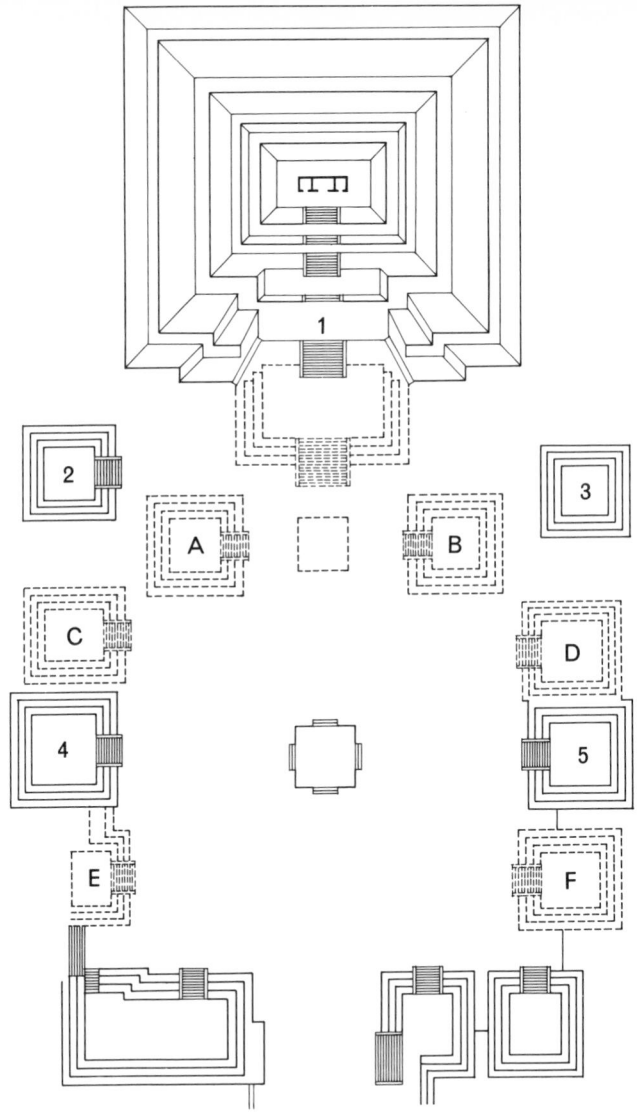

Plan of the Square of the Moon at Teotihuacan. The dotted lines indicate constructions erected during a second stage

group of platforms was constructed in successive stages.

If we compare this sacred ensemble to a cathedral its function will become clearer: in the center, and on a higher level than the rest of the ensemble, is the choir and high altar. In the Square of the Moon this corresponds to the great pyramid with its forepart. Surrounding it are the twelve smaller pyramids or platforms which at one time were surmounted by sanctuaries; they correspond to the secondary altars found in the chapels bordering the aisles of a cathedral.

The organization is undoubtedly hierarchical. The high priest officiating at the high altar is echoed by the numerous priests who led worship on the summits of the smaller pyramids enclosing the square in which the 'congregation' assembled.

The Citadel

The Square of the Moon was built in successive stages; but the plan of the large quadrangular enclosure known as the Citadel was apparently based on a single concept. Its structure precluded any later modifications – although some buildings, such as the centrally placed Temple of Quetzalcoatl, were added to.

Basically, the Citadel consists of a great quadrilateral, 1320 feet along one side, formed by an embankment 10 feet high and between 100 and 300 feet wide. This encloses a courtyard measuring 643.5 by 775.5 feet. The complex is built on a west-east axis, and two sides and one end are surmounted by a second embankment as high as the first, in the shape of a horse-shoe, and supporting four small platforms or pyramids placed laterally to the north and south. Four other platforms are built on the single-storeyed front embankment which, by means of a broad monumental staircase, gives access to the quadrilateral. At the far end is the pyramid-temple of Quetzalcoatl, behind which are three small platforms placed symmetrically along the main axis.

The platforms enclosing the square all have paneled construction and two or three superimposed levels. In the center of the courtyard is a small, square, single-storeyed platform with a staircase on each of its four sides.

As in the Square of the Moon, but with greater discipline, the sense of perfect organization is achieved by means of remarkably straightforward plastic elements. The controlled formal vocabulary imposes a play of horizontal rhythms which suggest both strength and subtlety. By repeating forms, by disciplined, orthogonal plans which result in the different square, cubed and paralleliped elements all being subjected to the same play of light and shadow, the pre-Columbians made the Citadel one of the most intense groups of buildings in world architecture. The breadth of the proportions, the feeling of open space, the deliberate art with which the perspectives are arranged so as to cause the surrounding air to vibrate within the negative volume of the quadrilateral, the harmony between walls and staircases whose flights stress the soaring lines – all contribute to make the Citadel one of man's major achievements. The simplest methods – embankments and platforms – have resulted in a moving sense of grandeur. What is more concise than a few embankments placed around a square, and animated by some fifteen small platforms? There is no recourse to internal play of space, to soaring columns or arches. Only a series of mounds arranged with extraordinary wisdom. That is all.

The Temple of Quetzalcoatl

During excavations on the site of the Citadel at the turn of the century, the most surprising finds were made in the center of the complex, the Temple of Quetzalcoatl. Beneath the pile of rubble – all that then remained of the temple – archeologists discovered a kind of forepart, consisting of four levels with a broad axial staircase leading to the summit. The construction was placed against a larger pyramid of six storeys. The forepart is about 165 feet wide, while the pyramid, square in plan, measures no more than 214.5 feet along one side.

Borings made before restoration revealed that the forepart had been superimposed on an earlier building; and the latter was found to have fine sculpted ornamentation in high and bas-relief on its panels. Due to superimposition, which had protected the sculptures from both time and man, the façade was almost perfectly preserved, and consequently could be detached intact.

The façade beneath indicates the level which Teotihuacan art reached at its height. It has none of the decorative formulae of other buildings on the site; no longer painted with simple frescoes, the panels are now carved with fine sculptures in relief; heads of the Plumed Serpent, Quetzalcoatl, are shown alternating with heads of the god of rain, Tlaloc. The first are represented by dragons with sharp fangs, fire-breathing jaws, and round eyes; the second are shown in geometrically stylized masks, with ringed eyes and discs in relief ornamenting the faces.

The heads alternate horizontally, along each panel, but are superimposed, the sculptures of Quetzalcoatl being placed directly over each other, and, similarly, those of Tlaloc. They form parallel vertical rows. These sculptures are incorporated into the framework projecting from the panels, and are set against a background consisting of meanders representing the Plumed Serpent and aquatic symbols such as shells and snails.

Originally these motifs decorated all four faces and six superimposed levels of the square pyramid. They were carved in hard stone which, in turn, was covered with a polychrome layer. In its complete state – including the twelve heads of Quetzalcoatl bordering the ramps of the great staircase – the monument probably had about 365 representations of gods, that is, equivalent to the number of days in one year.

The small platform in the center of the quadrilateral had a similar symbolical significance, for its four staircases each have thirteen steps, a total of 52. In pre-Columbian times this number corresponded to a cycle of 52 years, equivalent to our century.

The constructional technique of the panels on the Temple of Quetzalcoatl is unusual in that they are not formed of the limestone mortar found everywhere else, but of large, accurately pointed stone blocks. The quality of the decoration is therefore equalled by that of the material. Even the foundations reveal a concern for quality: the bulk of the pyramid rests on intersecting pillars and buttresses that form cells – rather like the cells of a honeycomb – filled with soil and stones. The structure is therefore stronger than that of the two great pyramids; perhaps Teotihuacan builders devoted so much care to this temple because it was especially sacred.

The systematic use of the panel over entire surfaces seems to have begun with the Temple of Quetzalcoatl. Here the system has clearly expanded and is, indeed, a constituent element of the whole pyramid. Thenceforward it was to be applied to all the platforms and pyramids in Teotihuacan. We may therefore assume that mortar construction was no more than a transposition of forms which had earlier been created in freestone, the only material then available for strong plastic effects, and to some extent foreign to, and even contrasting with the fragile mortar usually employed in Teotihuacan buildings.

Another development comes to light in the study of the Temple of Quetzalcoatl: that of the forepart or front section of a monument. The preservation of most of the decoration of the early face of the pyramid can only be accounted for by the four storeyed platform built against it. We have already encountered this feature in the pyramids of the Sun and the Moon, but here it assumes an even greater significance since it is almost as large as the pyramid itself. A comparison of the pyramids shows that the relation of volume between the forepart and the main building continually increased: the proportion for the pyramid of the Sun is $1/250$; for the pyramid of the Moon it is $1/30$; and it almost reaches $1/3$ in the Temple of Quetzalcoatl.

The palaces of the priests

A whole living area has come to light in the Citadel, located on either side of the Temple of Quetzalcoatl. It consists of the palaces once occupied by the priesthood who tended the sanctuaries. Because they were inside the enclosure these buildings might have been relatively insignificant, for their height never exceeded that of the embankments surrounding the quadrilateral. None the less they cover an area of some 54,000 square feet. Despite the fragmentary state of the remains, we can still distinguish a building in patio form south of the pyramid; the form was typical of numerous buildings in Teotihuacan, and can be found in the suburbs at Tetitla, Atetelco, Tepantitla, Xolapan, as well as in the area known as the Viking Group, near the Causeway of the Dead, and even in the Palace of Quetzalpapalotl, recently restored and which we have mentioned in connection with the chronological information it provides.

The cruciform shaped building with its patio, is based on a centripetal composition – rooms face into the rectangular or square courtyard and not outwards – and is characteristic of Teotihuacan architecture. It was to be perpetuated in a number of civilizations on the high plateaux.

The Palace of Quetzalpapalotl

The Palace of Quetzalpapalotl provides an excellent example of civil architecture in Teotihuacan. For the first time we see a building, designed purely as living quarters for the city's dignitaries, completely restored. Patient research and careful reconstruction has resulted in the building regaining its original appearance, and we can now visualize daily life in the great capital of the central Meseta.

For this reason the Palace deserves special consideration. It was discovered in 1962, during Professor Bernal's excavations on the site of the Square of the Moon. It was in fact the entrance to the building which was found in the south-west corner of the Square (close to platform E). A staircase of about fifteen steps and 59.4 feet wide leads to a vestibule in the form of a hypostyle hall, its façade consisting of a five-pillared portico surmounted by a paneled frieze. The hall (39.6 feet by 33 feet) has a flat roof supported by four square pillars and, through a small horizontal door, opens onto the east gallery of the Palace. This consists of a portico opening onto

Plan of the palaces of the Viking group, lining the Causeway of the Dead

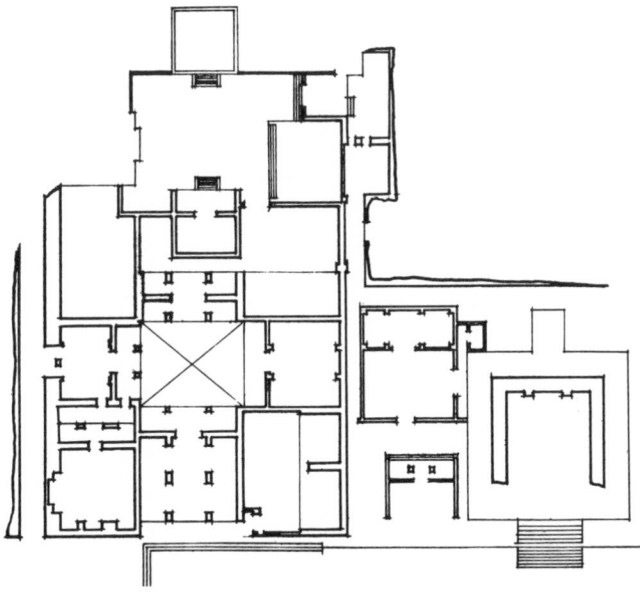

101

the patio, a kind of Roman impluvium, encircled by stone pillars. The central courtyard, 33 by 24.6 feet, is symmetrical in plan; a gallery extends for a short distance behind the portico to the south, west and north. Behind the gallery, on each of the three sides of the portico, are rooms, 26.4 to 28.7 feet by 22.1 feet. Both the gallery and the rooms have flat roofs with a framework of joists embedded in limestone mortar. The courtyard floor is entirely covered by a layer of stucco, sloping slightly towards the center where there is an opening for a drain leading to a cistern which stored water caught on the roofs during the rainy season.

Surmounting the gallery around the patio was a frieze of stucco and polychrome panels depicting traditional Teotihuacan motifs. The frieze itself was surmounted by a series of flat stones – as in the sanctuaries – dressed above each column, forming crenels whose function was purely decorative.

Perhaps the most interesting feature of the Palace is the magnificent freestone pillars, carved with fine bas-reliefs. The sculptures consist of mythical animals, a cross between Quetzal birds and butter-

The entrance to the hypostyle hall leading to the palace of Quetzalpapalotl at Teotihuacan

flies, sometimes depicted full-face and sometimes in profile. The name of the Palace derives from these bas-reliefs.

The surfaces are further animated by obsidian incrustations on the eyes of the animals and on shells symbolizing water, and were at one time painted in vivid colors. The pillars were either rectangular or, in the angles of the building, square, and had been carved after the blocks were set in position. This accounts for the accuracy of the reconstruction; despite the numerous decorative elements each stone can occupy only one position.

We must stress the purely functional nature of Teotihuacan palaces. Because of the amount of sun on the high plateaux the need for shade was paramount. The covered galleries that led to the rooms – which were very dark, light penetrating only through doors sometimes over six feet wide – gave protection from the harsh sun and kept the rooms cool.

The arrangement of rooms in palace annexes clearly shows that builders were chiefly concerned with providing practical quarters: rooms are often freely distributed around a center formed by the patio and the principal ceremonial chambers. The rooms were connected by a complicated series of corridors, but were set out according to a strict orthogonal plan; each building forms a distinct 'island.' As in Rome, each had a patio, together with 'living-rooms,' store-rooms, warehouses and workshops.

In addition to the porticos, the ceremonial chambers were often decorated in rich colors. Generally the paintings are found on a kind of raised bench that ran around the rooms and the length of the galleries. These frescoes have provided much valuable information about the daily life of both dignitaries and ordinary citizens during the classical period. Many more frescoes have come to light during recent excavations at Teotihuacan, thus increasing our knowledge. Their beauty indicates how great an aesthetic sense the ruling classes possessed. The palace surrounding the sacred center have a splendor that equals the finest villas found at Pompeii. They testify to an extremely refined way of life, and this is one of the more important contributions that excavations have made to our knowledge of pre-Columbians.

Fresco depicting a Quetzal bird

Fresco depicting a coiffed jaguar

Divinities evidently occupied a primary place in this pictorial repertory. Animals and mythical creatures such as the coiffed jaguar, the Plumed Serpent and Tlaloc, are the most commonly depicted; but there are also innumerable scenes of worship, ceremonies, and representations of temples and sanctuaries. Religion is depicted in a kind of everlasting paradise, a Garden of Eden bathed in running waters, where the fortunate enjoy a better life. Some paintings are almost true-to-life, with jaguars hunting multicolored birds through the undergrowth.

It is worth noting at this point that a marked similarity of style exists between the paintings of Teotihuacan and those at Tajin. Teotihuacan frescoes reveal characteristics of Totonac bas-reliefs, leading us to assume that there were close connections between the two cities before the Christian era. The full significance of these connections will, however, only come to light when excavations now in progress at Tajin are completed.

The ball-court

In our survey of La Venta we suggested that the two long embankments situated near the pyramid may well have marked the limits of one of the earliest pre-Columbian ball-courts. However, there are no signs at Teotihuacan – although a later city than La Venta – of ball-courts similar to those found at Tajin, and the Mayan capitals of Copan, Uxmal, etc. How can this omission be explained? In fact, a recently covered – and still not widely known – fresco depicts a very unusual form of the game. Luis Aveleyra Arroyo de Anda, a Mexican archeologist, was the first to prove that the game existed at Teotihuacan, but in a different form. His proof is based on evidence provided by a curious stone carving, over six feet high with its base – the base was discovered after the publication of Aveleyra's theory in 'La Estela teotihuacan de La Ventilla,' (1963). The stele consisted of four parts: cylindrical, drum-shaped, globe-shaped and circular, the last resembling a disc placed vertically on its edge. According to Aveleyra, the stele was a 'goal post' used in the Teotihuacan ball game, and the four sections were joined by means of tenons.

After careful research Aveleyra found additional fragments of goal posts; he also made a revealing comparison between his discovery and a fresco at Tepantitla which shows players in action, carrying bats (rather like baseball bats). At either end of the pitch are goal posts similar to the stele found at La Ventilla. Here the shaft is surmounted by a vertically placed disc which served as a target. Although parts of the fresco have been obliterated, it seems as though there were about twelve members to a side, not including the goalkeepers who are represented horizontally, together with their goal posts. The discs crowning the stelae each bear an insignia – probably the teams' 'colors.' This would account for the perforated motif in the center of the Ventilla disc.

Before the stele was found, fragments of similar goalposts (discs, cylindrical pieces attached to shafts, etc.) had been discovered, particularly along the Causeway of the Dead. Should we therefore assume that the game was played on sections of this avenue, with boundaries marked by the staircases or horizontal panels that intersect the perspective? This is possible. The courts would be situated on the axis of the pyramid of the Moon. It follows that special constructions would not be necessary since parts of the Causeway served the purpose. This axial plan can, furthermore, be compared to the plan at La Venta. Indeed, it was to remain unchanged until the end of the pre-Columbian world; in the Aztecs' capital, Tenochtitlan, the area reserved for the

Stele of La Ventilla: similar 'goalposts' were set at either end of the ballcourt at Teotihuacan

sacred game was situated on the axis of the Templo Major and the Temple of Quetzalcoatl.

The architectural development of the Teotihuacan ball-court was never as extensive as that of the lowlands. This is not surprising, for we know the game originated in jungle regions where latex for the rubber balls could be found. The lowland origins are further confirmed by the ornamentation on the Ventilla stele, which is Totonac in style: the interlacings and volutes clearly reveal the influence of bas-reliefs at Tajin.

It is tempting to suggest that the game as played during Toltec and Aztec periods developed from a combination of two different forms: one characterized by horizontal embankments, the other by discs surmounting goalposts. The discs would develop into rings placed halfway between the teams, on the horizontal walls or embankments bordering the pitch. In the Teotihuacan form of the game, the ball was aimed at, and rebounded from the center of the target-discs at either end of the field; but when the goals were moved to the sides of the field, between the two teams, the ball could pass through the target, which then automatically became an open ring. According to this theory, the two poles of pre-Columbian civilization – the high plateaux and the lowlands near the Gulf of Mexico – would therefore be responsible for a ball-court based on two different forms of the game.

The Causeway of the Dead

The great processional avenue, named the Causeway of the Dead by sixteenth-century Spanish historians, is about 1¼ miles long and 132 feet wide. It passes through the sacred ensemble of Teotihuacan – from the Citadel to the Square of the Moon – with a slight rise in level, about 1½ per cent. The Square of the Moon is therefore approximately 100 feet higher than the Citadel. Instead of constructing the avenue on an even slope, Teotihuacan architects divided it into broad flights of steps which accentuate its

rhythm. There are eight 'landings,' rising gradually from south to north, and seven flights of steps enable the spectator to look out over the Causeway. Since there was no wheeled traffic, the steps presented no problems.

The arrangement of the steps took into account the groups of buildings lining either side of the Causeway. Progress to the pyramid of the Sun, for example, is unimpeded for more than 1000 feet. On the other hand, in the area of the Viking Group, the total distance between two landings is often less than 300 feet; and it was here that fragments of stelae used in the ball-game were discovered. This may therefore have been one of the pitches, with boundaries formed by a staircase at either end, and platforms along both sides.

Right and left of the Causeway are small pyramids of two, three and four levels, together with staircases giving access to higher platforms. Consequently the avenue was not merely a long clear vista, but a carefully planned space, bordered by low buildings which served to stress the long perspectives.

Town planning

The Causeway of the Dead leads us to consider the plan of the city. We are concerned here only with the sacred center and the palaces of the dignitaries, for there are no traces left of the dwellings of ordinary citizens, which, in any case, probably resembled the huts in which millions of Indians still live. However, archeologists have estimated that if, during the city's greatest period, the ceremonial center covered an area of 1.6 square miles and the palaces an area of 9.3 square miles, the other buildings must have spilled over into the plain. The area of the whole city must therefore have been about 12½ square miles.

Evidence of deliberate planning can be seen everywhere. The ruling element is the Causeway of the Dead, extending right across the city, and lined by various groups of buildings. The position of the avenue is linked with astronomy and reflects mathematical precision. For some time archeologists have known that it is not, in fact, oriented on a south-north line but deviates slightly by 17 degrees to the east in regard to the astronomical north. The deviation seems to have been deliberate and has a cosmological significance: the latitude of Teotihuacan is over 4 degrees south of the Tropic of Cancer, and here the sun reaches its zenith twice a year (May 16 ascending, and July 26 descending). As we have noted, the sun played a major role in Teotihuacan culture, so these dates must have been specially celebrated. Moreover the position of places of worship clearly reveals this.

The chief face of the pyramid of the Sun, therefore, is oriented directly towards the point where the sun disappears over Teotihuacan on these two dates. The Causeway of the Dead is placed perpendicularly to the imaginary axis linking the summit of the pyramid to this point. Since all the buildings followed a strictly orthogonal plan, thenceforward the whole city was ruled by this orientation, based on a well-defined religious system.

The great avenue forms a straight south-north line along which the whole city was to be arranged. It rises slightly to culminate in the Square of the Moon, blocked by the pyramid outlined against Cerro Gordo, a mountain that cuts off the northern horizon.

We have noted that symmetry rules the arrangement of groups of buildings, so the Causeway cannot form the main axis of the city since it is responsible for a symmetrical plan only at its finishing point in the Square of the Moon. The huge groups such as the Citadel and the pyramid of the Sun with its satellite altars are, on the contrary, situated on the east side of the Causeway.

The sacred buildings are built on perpendicular axes: pyramids and esplanades are arranged symmetrically as regards their own axes, but asymmetrically in relation to the Causeway. The exception is the Square of the Moon which, as it were, straddles the Causeway. Although the overall plan cannot be reduced to an axial formula, each group of buildings conforms to its own pattern; we can compare them to constellations, every one of which has its individual gravitation.

This strict plan extends beyond the actual sacred complex, and governs the structure of neighboring areas. This is shown by aerial photographs which also indicate a division of land similar to that of the Romans, with a fixed orientation. Each pyramid has its dependent platforms, each square its esplanades, each ensemble its well-defined limits governed by right-angles. The plan is strengthened by a kind of polarization; and while its chief characteristic may be economy of means, this is balanced by the use of skilful solutions and a variety of combinations. Within the laws of orthogonality and symmetry, all possibilities have apparently been exploited.

In the face of this all-encompassing system how can we account for the fact that the town as a whole lacked a symmetrical plan based on an axis formed by the Causeway of the Dead? Despite their wish for strict symmetry, it seems that Teotihuacan architects wanted to avoid such a system, which would have required either the repetition of all features on both sides of the Causeway, or doing away with the very original central section of the Causeway. Probably, the philosophico-religious concepts of the Teotihuacans were not founded on static dualism: their 'weltanschauung' was, rather, dynamic and dialectic. This, at any rate, is the impression that results from a thorough study of the plan of Teotihuacan.

According to the plan, the pyramid of the Sun –although it is the most important feature of the ensemble– was deliberately placed on the east side of the Causeway of the Dead. This suggests that the

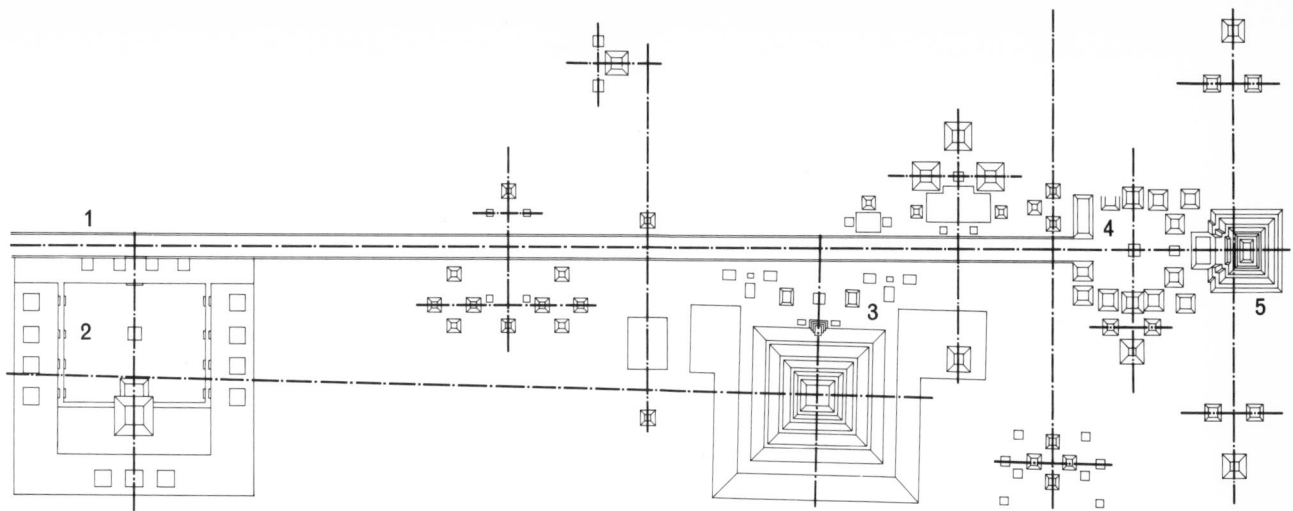

Town plan, showing the principal axes along which Teotihuacan was constructed. 1 Causeway of the Dead. 2 The Citadel. 3 The pyramid of the Sun. 4 The Square of the Moon. 5 The pyramid of the Moon

Causeway is not an axis, but a vector, its guiding function further stressed by its ascending slope. Similarly, the location of the Citadel does not balance the plan since it, too, is built east of the Causeway.

Professor Horst Hartung, whose evaluation of the plan of Teotihuacan is both extensive and revealing, emphasizes the complementary link between the pyramid of the Sun and the Citadel. Indeed, it is a negative and positive relationship: the pyramid, which forms a projecting mass, a volume in relief, is counteracted by the quadrilateral with its concave space surrounded by the quadrangular walls of the Citadel. Furthermore, only one line leads from the summit and descends parallel to the Causeway, and this passes through the exact geometric center of the Citadel. Is this coincidence? We do not think so. The plan of the city is so complete that it is difficult to imagine such connections are purely accidental. The dialogue of negative and positive

has, moreover, been shown in Mayan town planning, more specifically in the pyramids and quadrilaterals of Uxmal.

Organic development

Growing from the trunk of a tree, represented by the principal avenue, are branches, consisting of the perpendicularly placed axes of the various groups of buildings. The analogy with nature helps to explain the axial arrangement of the Square of the Moon: even when branches grow horizontally from the trunk of a conifer, its summit still continues as an extension of the trunk. This applies to the structure of a leaf, with its ribs and veins branching out in all directions. The Causeway of the Dead, then, is branched by perspectives opening out to the east and west, where perpendicular constructions in turn give birth to other complexes, all based on a strictly orthogonal alternation. We are obviously dealing with an organic growth. The city plan is open to unlimited development by the addition of architectural elements governed by individual symmetry, but place asymmetrically along the Causeway.

The systematized plan of Teotihuacan did not come about accidentally – any more than it ended accidentally. New constructions could be added without interfering in the balance of the rest of the city. In this respect, the strength of Teotihuacan townplanning forecasted a future urban pattern, ruled by principles which allowed for every solution compatible with the basic plan. In this theocracy, the corollary to authority and hierarchy did not do away with freedom. The plan did not impose insurmountable outlines, nor a framework that had to be shattered, nor limits that had to be broken in order to proceed to the next stage.

There exists, on the contrary, an architectonic dialectic which can be expressed in the repeated use of elements complete within themselves yet forming part of a freely developing system.

At Teotihuacan, the pre-Columbians provided an answer to the question of alternatives which dog town-planning everywhere: restraint or anarchy. The plan of Teotihuacan reveals considerable freedom of improvization, although within the limits set by a wholly consistent structure. The limits are apparent in the principles of the plan and not in any ruling outline which would prevent any form of development. Teotihuacan's plan is dynamic and provides a valuable lesson, for it is based on real organic growth, thus anticipating the most daring solutions of our time by some two thousand years.

Lack of fortifications

The freedom of Teotihuacan town planning also indicates the peacefulness and stability of the period in which the city was built. A kind of 'pax Teotihuacan' must have reigned, and this is clear from the lack of any form of fortification. The authority of the priests over the surrounding territory was apparently so great that outside threats seemed inconceivable.

The security of this people, whose life centred around worship of the gods, was expressed in a magnificent body of masterpieces. Yet their security was also the Achilles heel of the city, for when the northern tribes attacked, Teotihuacan was powerless to resist. It had been in existence for nearly eight centuries, and its annihilation was as sudden as it was unexpected.

Chronology of Teotihuacan

What were the stages of its development? Contemporary chronology based on Carbon 14 analyses of joists and door-frames in the palace of Quetzalpapalotl show that previously accepted dates must be backdated by 200 or 250 years.

We can therefore assume that Teotihuacan dates from about the 4th century B.C. The core of the pyramid of the Sun probably dates from this first period, which ended about 250 B.C. The two great pyramids, together with the Causeway of the Dead, date from about the 2nd century B.C. During this second period, Teotihuacan II, the first stage of the Square of the Moon, the Temple of Quetzalcoatl, and the structure of the Citadel were constructed. In Teotihuacan III, the 1st and 2nd centuries, the panel system of construction became widespread; this period saw the completion of the Square of the Moon, the enclosure of the Citadel, and the construction of a series of magnificent palaces bordering the Causeway of the Dead. The palace of Quetzalpapalotl dates from Teotihuacan III A, the beginning or the middle of the 3rd century A.D. Two hundred years later northern invaders systematically destroyed the sacred center and the palaces. Between 450 A.D. and 650 A.D. (Teotihuacan IV) the city still existed, but it was finally abandoned following a fresh invasion.

Notes

Tajin

Tajin, near the Gulf of Mexico, still conceals some hundred unexplored monuments and, perhaps, will provide archeologists with their greatest finds. Payon has been excavating the site for some thirty years, and the number of architectural forms that have come to light is remarkable. It was here that pre-Columbian builders gave full reign to their genius. Yet tropical vegetation had buried most of the remains and the work of restoration and reconstruction was enormous.

The only visible and known monument before systematic excavation was begun was the pyramid of the Niches – and it was only discovered in 1780. Recently, restoration necessitated the breaking up of several storeys; torrential rains flooded the monument and it was in danger of being completely destroyed. Tajin buildings, like most in Mexico, were constructed with a core of beaten earth (adobes) surrounded by a layer of stone cemented with easily destroyed mortar.

The pyramid is the best constructed of all buildings on the site. Its large basalt blocks have served as protection against total destruction. Other monuments, constructed with the minimum of dressing or, even more simply, by juxtaposing shapeless blocks embedded deep in mortar, have been undermined by the vegetation. Reconstruction is therefore a laborious task. That is partly why it will be a long time before Tajin is restored to its former splendor.

The pyramid of the Niches has 365 niches, the number of days in the year. The pre-Columbian used a double calendar: the ritual period of 260 days, divided into 13 months each with 20 days, and the solar year of 365 days, divided into 18 months also with 20 days a month, plus five days considered unlucky. The two calendars only coincided once every 52 years. The latter was the equivalent of our century. This system governed numerous architectonic creations. There are many buildings which were begun on a date corresponding to the first day of the new cycle. Thus the connection between architecture and the calendar, between sanctuaries and astronomy, remained a constant in the pre-Columbian world.

Xochicalco

The constructional methods of numerous complexes in the Totonac capital seem rudimentary, and those of a great many monuments at Xochicalco – excepting the pyramid of Quetzalcoatl which is finely dressed – are similar. Indifferently quarried roughstone was used to build temples, pyramids, platforms and even square and rectangular pillars. A series of buildings forming the sacred ensemble at Xochicalco was recently brought to light by Cesar Saenz. Noteworthy is complex A which surmounts the temple of the Stelae, where excavations revealed magnificent and finely carved monoliths.

Tula

Excavation and restoration at Tula has been chiefly concerned with the pyramid of Tlahuizcalpantecuhtli. The basalt Atlases that supported the now disappeared sanctuary on the summit have been replaced. For a long time these magnificent sculptures – one a copy, the original being in the Museo de Antropologia at Mexico City – were lost, buried at the foot of the monument. Today they may be enjoyed in their original setting.

Tula also brought to light the prototype of statuary which was to spread as far as Chichen Itza. This is the Chac-Mool. It consists of a human figure in full relief lying back, supported by the elbows, and with head erect; on the stomach is a platter carved in relief on which offerings made by Toltec priests were placed. This type of sculpture originated in the high plateaux, but it was to achieve most success during the period when the Toltecs fused with the Mayans of Yucatan. The Chac-Mool discovered in the Castillo sanctuary at Chichen Itza is infinitely more elaborate than the crude, almost brutal, effigies of Tula. On the other hand, in the temple of the Warriors, the magnificent pillars in the shape of Atlases have disappeared, and in their place are square-sectioned supports, identical to those in the second row, behind the four colossal basalt figures at Tula.

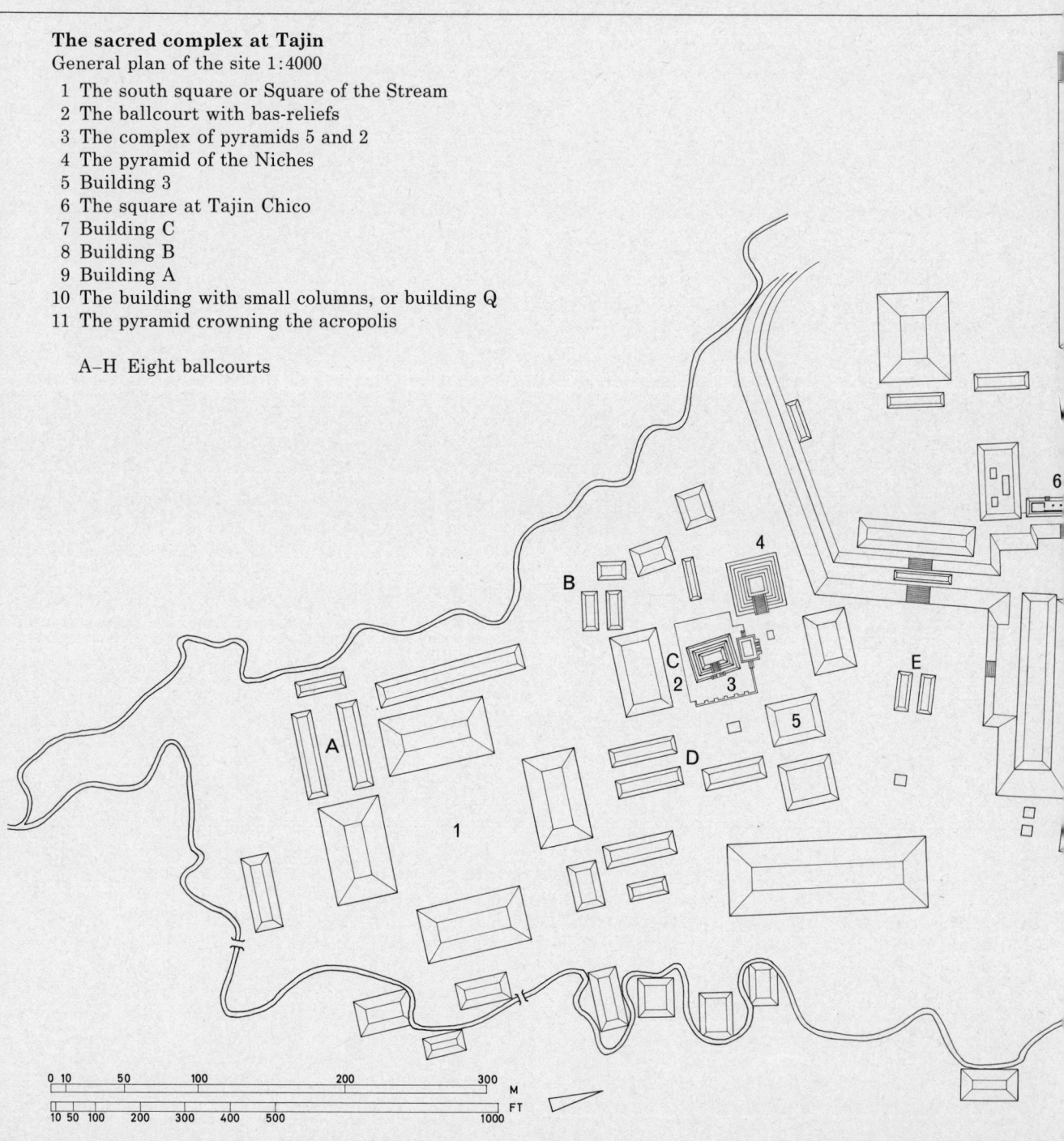

The sacred complex at Tajin
General plan of the site 1:4000

1 The south square or Square of the Stream
2 The ballcourt with bas-reliefs
3 The complex of pyramids 5 and 2
4 The pyramid of the Niches
5 Building 3
6 The square at Tajin Chico
7 Building C
8 Building B
9 Building A
10 The building with small columns, or building Q
11 The pyramid crowning the acropolis

A–H Eight ballcourts

Plates

Tajin (Veracruz)

113 Tajin seen from a helicopter: the vast ceremonial center, stripped of trees, is covered with tumuli. In the foreground, the south square surrounded by four connected pyramids. At left, the pyramid of the Niches and two constructions recently unearthed by Prof. Payon. Below, Tajin Chico, or Lesser Tajin.

114 A stele erected on the staircase of pyramid no. 5. The interlacing and volute ornamentation is typical of Totonac sculpture.

115 The pyramid of the Niches: including the motifs beneath the monumental staircase, there are 365 niches, that is to say, the number of days in the solar year. The lower part of the panels are bordered by a embankment and the upper part by a projecting cornice.

116 Bas-relief decorating the north wall of the ballcourt to the south of pyramid no. 5. The very fine late Totonac decoration depicts a human sacrifice performed by cardiectomy. Armed with a silex knife, the priest is about to officiate, while his acolyte holds down the victim. At right, a seated dignitary.

117 Buildings C and B at Tajin Chico. Pyramid C, consisting of three storeys, is decorated with niches.

118 Building C, with its high mounds and key-pattern alcoves, surmounted by broad projecting cornices.

119 Detail of volute motifs decorating the partition-walls of the staircase scaling the east side of building C.

Xochicalco (Morelos)

120 The principal square in the sacred center at Xochicalco. At right, building A that surmounts the temple of Stelae, recently restored and excavated by Cesar Saenz. In the background, the pyramid of Quetzalcoatl.

121 The pyramid of Quetzalcoatl encircled by meanders of the Plumed Serpent. The second storey must have supported a flat-roofed sanctuary.

Plans

122 Detail of the north-east corner of the building, with a head of a Plumed Serpent. At left, a symbol representing a date in the astronomical calendar.

Tula (Hidalgo)

123 The pyramid of Tlahuizcalpantecuhtli, god of the morning star. This five-storeyed building, preceded by a huge hypostyle hall, was surmounted by a sanctuary of which only the supports of the roof remain: Atlases and square pillars. The construction and plan of this pyramid resembles that of the temple of Warriors at Chichen Itza (Yucatan), a Mayan-Toltec creation.

124 Preserved by a later superimposition, a part of the decoration of the two lower storeys of the pyramid has remained untouched. On a steeply inclined base, a first frieze formed of skewbacks depicts pairs of eagles devouring hearts and jaws of Plumed Serpents (seen full-face) from which emerge human heads. The upper frieze is decorated with passant jaguars.

125 Above, detail of a passant jaguar, in stuccoed bas-relief. The captive beast is depicted wearing a collar. Below, a panel showing two eagles devouring the hearts of sacrificial victims.

126 Detail of a basalt Atlas representing a Toltec warrior with feathered headdress. He carries a breastplate depicting a butterfly.

127 Four Toltec warriors carved in relief supported the roofing of the sanctuary of the pyramid dedicated to Tlahuizcalpantecuhtli. Four square pillars in the middle ground are also decorated with warriors, sculpted in bas-relief. The entrance was divided into three bays, by means of two circular columns that at one time must have had at their bases the head of Plumed Serpents, as in the temple of the Warriors at Chichen Itza.

128 Three hypostyle halls with patios, today ruined, flanked the pyramids to the west. Here the warriors of the Toltec orders of the Eagle and Jaguar assembled.

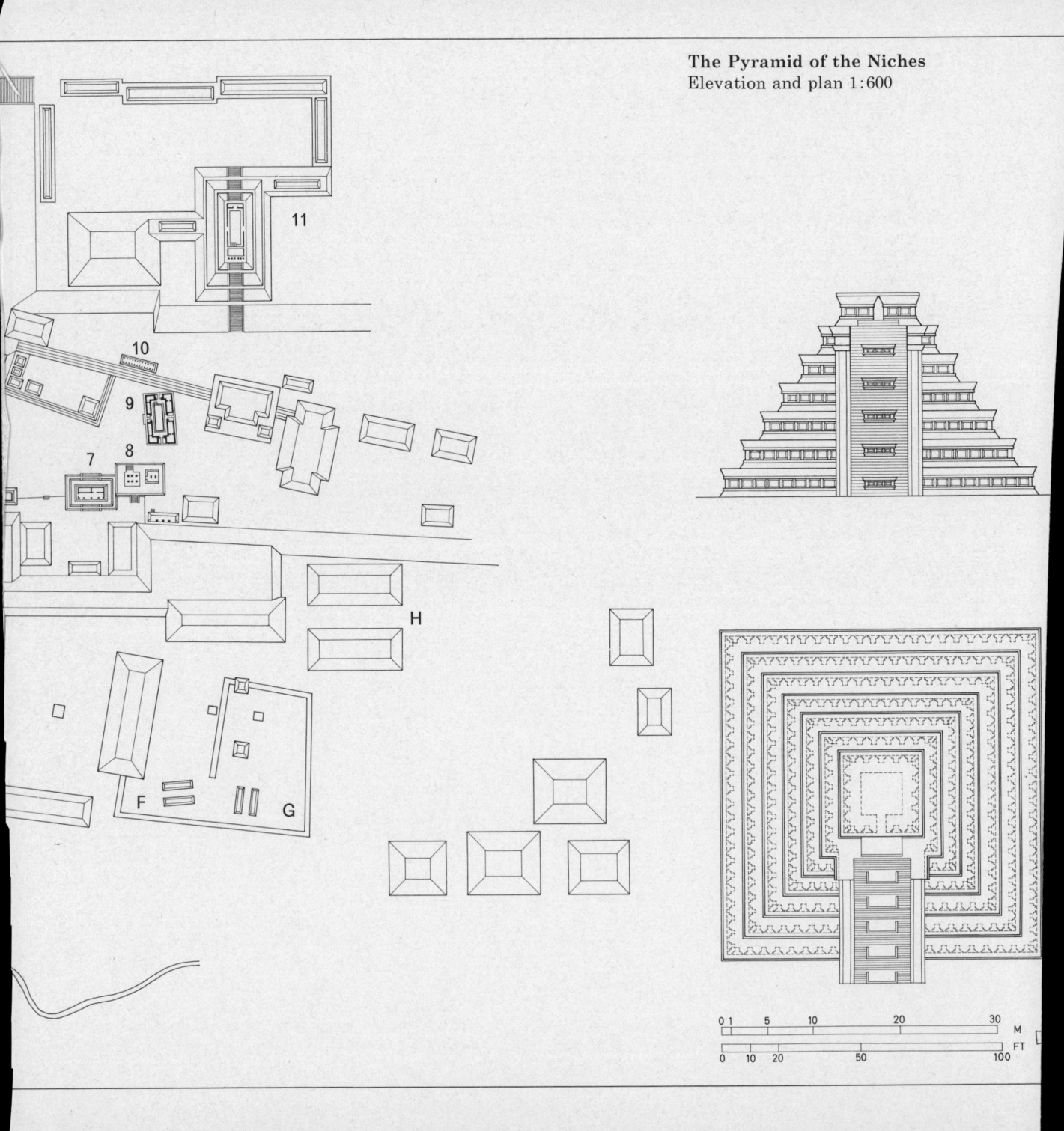

11

10

9

8

7

H

F

G

0 1 5 10 20 30 M

0 10 20 50 100 FT

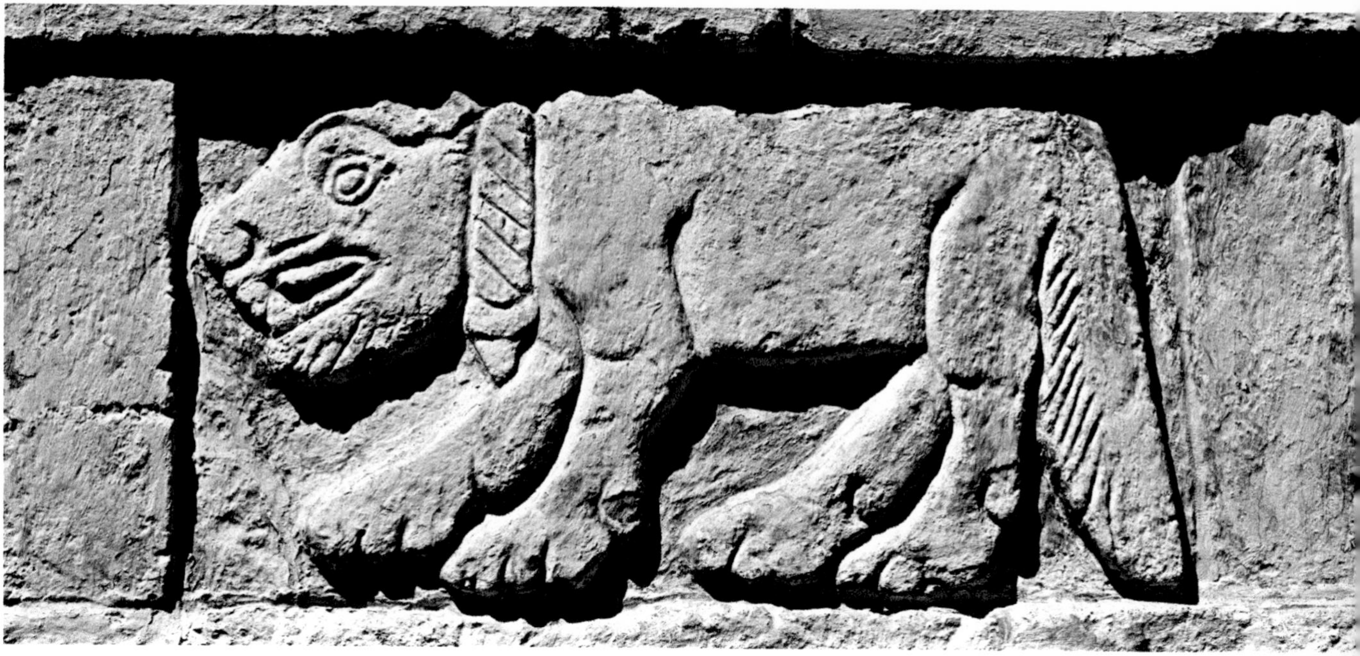

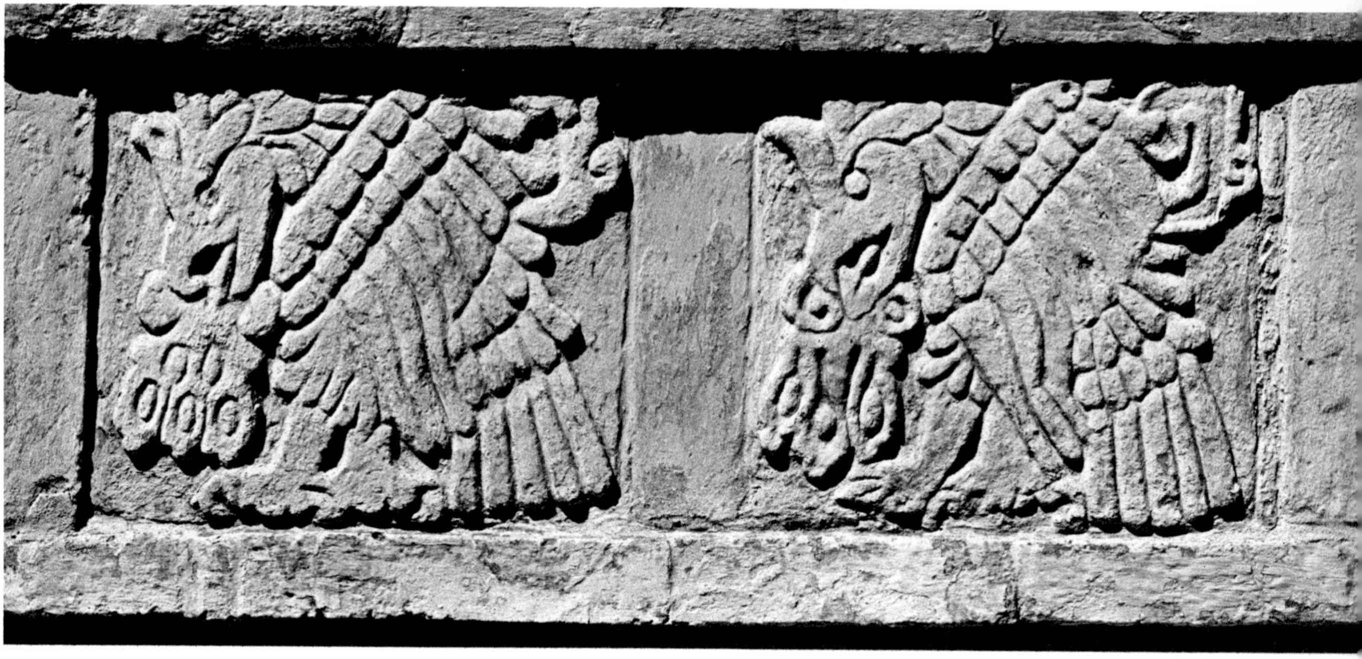

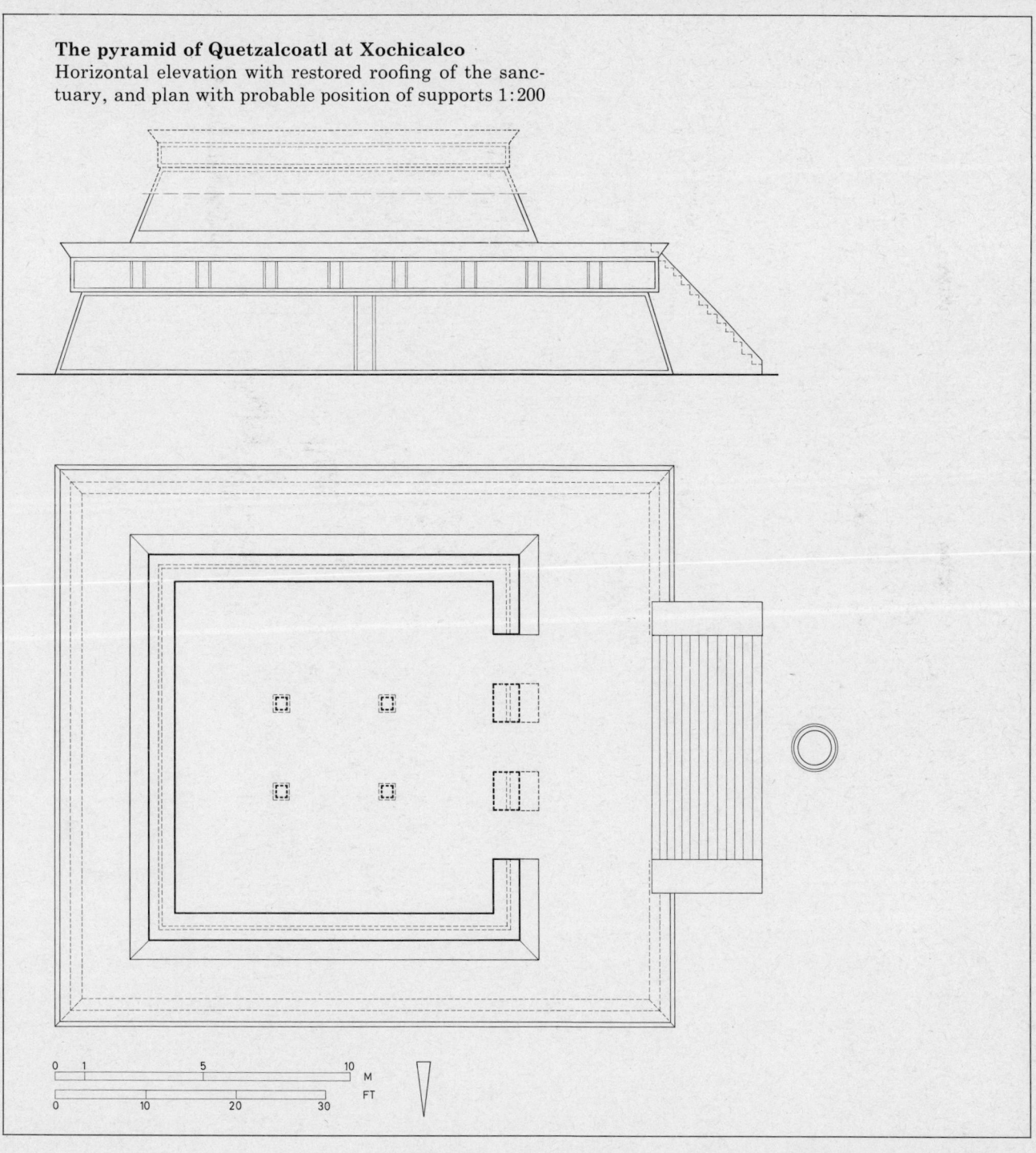

The pyramid of Quetzalcoatl at Xochicalco
Horizontal elevation with restored roofing of the sanctuary, and plan with probable position of supports 1:200

0 1   5   10   M

0   10   20   30   FT

The central complex at Tula

Restored elevation of pyramid B, or temple of Tlahuizcal-pantecuhtli, and plan of excavated buildings 1:1000

1/3 The hypostyle halls with patio
 4 The pyramid of Tlahuizcalpantecuhtli
 5 The hypostyle hall
 6 A small hypostyle hall with patio
 7 The central altar (destroyed)
 8 The principal pyramid, or Building C

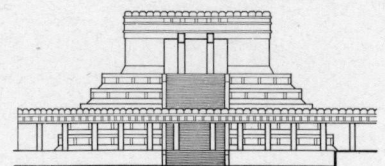

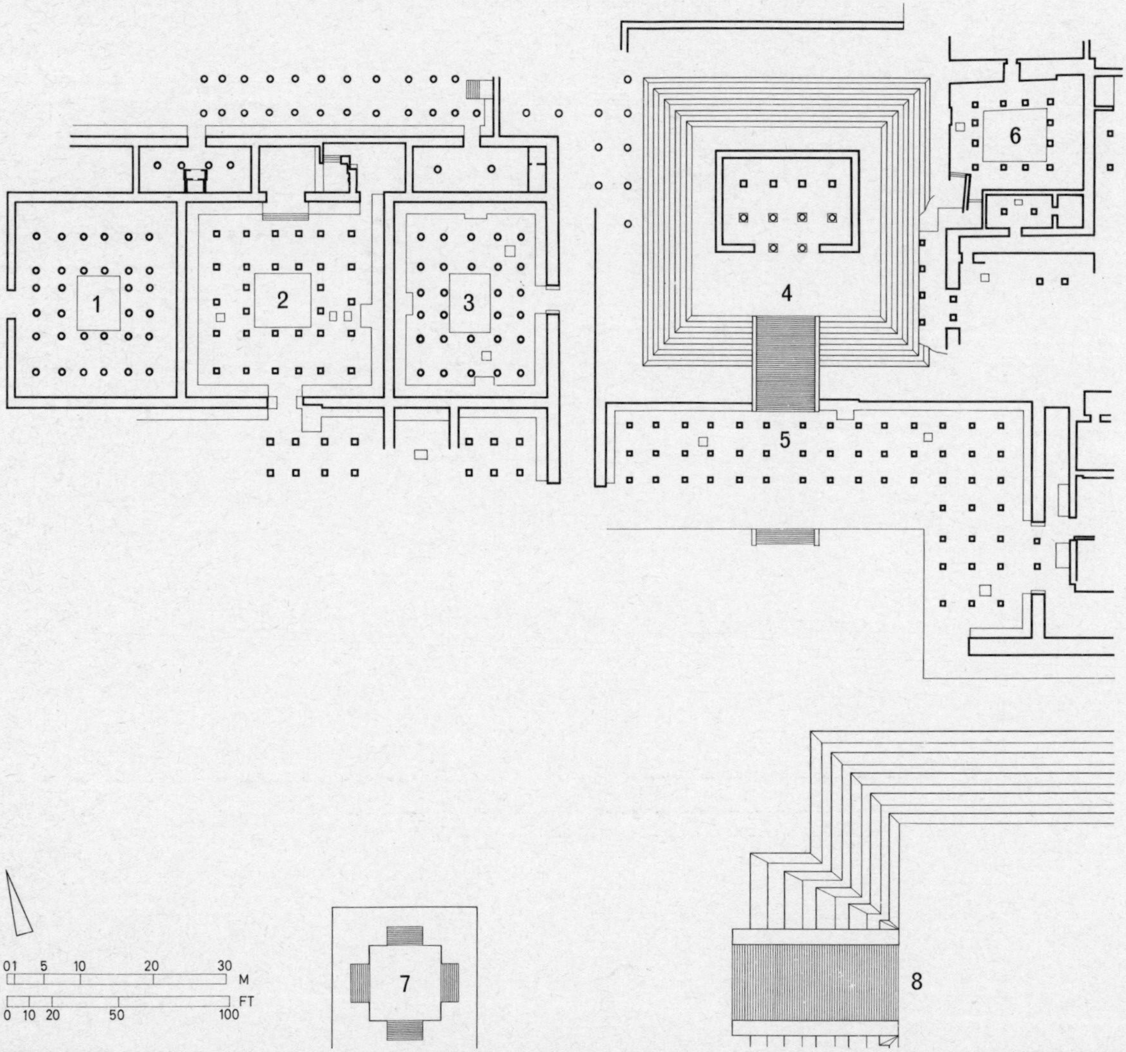

4. The Great builders of Southern Mexico and the Gulf

The city of Teotihuacan, which influenced all neighboring regions, has shown us that architecture on the high plateaux of the central Meseta developed at a very early period. However, there were other Mexican civilizations about this time whose magnificent creations contributed as much to the history of art. Everything in the pre-Columbian world resulted from influences and counter-influences; Middle American civilizations were closely related, despite different climates and geographical conditions, and despite the different uses necessitated by the individual materials of each region.

It seems that all pre-Columbian architectural forms stemmed from one principle, a constant that leads us through the labyrinth of ancient Mexican civilizations. Architectural unity is, in fact, only the outward and visible evidence of the strong cultural links that existed among apparently very different peoples. The connections between Teotihuacan and Monte Alban are particularly striking; their cultures developed almost simultaneously and in similar stages. For this reason we will stress both the resemblances and the differences between the two architectural forms – forms that played an equally important role in pre-Columbian classical art.

Monte Alban, sacred acropolis

Sacred capital of the Zapotecs, Monte Alban, the 'White Mountain,' lies in the center of the State of Oaxaca, about 220 miles south-east of Mexico City. It is a region of tortuous mountains intersected by deep valleys. The barren hill that is Monte Alban is situated at the junction of three fertile plains and is 1300 feet above the baroque city of Oaxaca, itself at an altitude of 5300 feet.

The Zapotec territory directly influenced by Monte Alban is located close to the isthmus of Tehuantepec, which marks the division between Mexican and Mayan cultural zones. Due to its situation the Zapotec civilization was not only a nucleus but also a crossroads for influences coming from the great pre-Columbian centers. It was therefore a zone of exchange, and its architectural role was to be specially significant, techniques and styles combining to produce highly original results.

Monte Alban stands in serene and splendid isolation on its hill-top; strategically, it is almost impregnable. Like Teotihuacan, with its lack of fortifications, it was primarily a center of worship. However, unlike the City of the Gods, built with apparent unconcern in the center of a plain, the capital of the Zapotecs crowns the summit of a steep hill.

The Mayans employed both sites for their cities (plains at Uxmal and Chichen Itza, Dzibilchaltun and Labna; hills at Tikal, San José, Piedras Nagras, Hochob, etc.). Monte Alban is, however, the clearest example of an attempt to build a sacred center on a site quite unsuitable to the development of a solidly structured urbanism. In fact the summit of the hill had to be leveled, hillocks and mounds flattened, retaining walls built, terracings laid out, perspectives corrected – a tremendous amount of work was necessary in order to construct the city.

The efforts of the whole tribe were concentrated on this unique and grandiose project, transforming a mountain into a sacred place of worship, and it clearly took centuries to complete. Monte Alban as it appears today is the fruit of more than a thousand years' labor. Most of the remains date from the period when the city was at its height, about the 8th century A.D. But Monte Alban III B ended about the close of the 8th century. However, we should remember that earlier constructions exist inside each building.

In this respect, the successive periods of Teotihuacan are almost contemporary with those of Monte Alban; the greatest architectural period of the City of the Gods, Teotihuacan III, corresponds to the Zapotec period of Monte Alban III (the 3rd to about the 6th centuries A.D.). Both regions have a similar chronology, revealed as much by ceramics as by architecture and painting. The relationship also existed with Tajin, on the Gulf of Mexico, whose pictorial motifs are often found in Zapotec paintings and frescoes.

Our survey of Monte Alban begins with an evaluation of the urban pattern during the city's greatest period of expansion. Reconstruction by Alfonso Caso, the 'father of Mexican archeology,' has restored the appearance of the great Zapotec capital at that time.

Town planning

The whole city extends for several miles over a chain of hills. The actual sacred center, however, is located in a well-defined area, on the upper part of the 'White Mountain.' It consists of an esplanade, approximately 2310 feet long by 825 feet wide. At the two extremities are pyramids, originally natural eminences which had been modeled by the Zapotecs. A vast square platform, 825 feet by 825 feet, encircled by various buildings, lies at the center.

The hill is oriented on an almost exact north-south line, and is crowned by a number of buildings whose positions indicate deliberate and strict planning: temples, pyramids and palaces were set out in an extremely interesting pattern. Some twenty buildings constitute the sacred center, which, because of its unusual location, seems isolated from the rest of the city; it is set between earth and sky, an island surrounded by the plain which, in turn, is encircled by mountains rising to over 10,000 feet.

Its extremities clearly marked to the north and south, the esplanade is bounded by sheer precipices on its east and west sides, whose straight lines are partially deliberate, the result of terracing and bold retaining walls. A series of buildings border the ravines on either side of the esplanade; broad staircases are built on their inner faces. Together with the northern and southern pyramids, also provided with staircases, the two rows of palaces and temples enclose a central area containing a building 330 feet long, oriented north-south, which marks the spine of the hill.

The interest of this arrangement lies in the play of elements: the esplanade is bordered on all sides by buildings backing onto space and facing the square. This is therefore a centripetal plan. However, the three buildings in the center, forming the line of intersection, are based on a centrifugal arrangement, with staircases and steps on both faces and extremities of the buildings.

While the row of buildings on the east side of the esplanade is set on a north-south line, the western row lies on a north-north-east to south-south-west line. The reason for this slight deflection (it does not exceed 6 degrees) is difficult to determine. But since three buildings are constructed on this line, two of which are identical sanctuaries (buildings M and System IV), the intention must have been deliberate; this becomes more apparent when we see that their orientation owes nothing to the natural contours, and it would even have been more straightforward to follow the outer limit of the esplanade, formed by the rectilinear ravine and oriented on an exact north-south line. Like Teotihuacan, where the 17° angle of the north-south axis is related to sunset on a particular date, the orientation of these buildings may have been based on a definite astronomical occurrence. In fact, the plan of these two buildings (M and System IV) alone seems to confirm this theory, for their pyramidal arrangement, with sanctuaries on the summits, is flanked on the east side by an enclosed courtyard reached by axial staircases; their function is therefore that of a plan, with a 'back sight' and a 'sight'. This can be clarified: due to the low quadrilateral enclosure in front of the eastern face of the pyramid, a priest standing on the staircase leading to the upper sanctuary could observe the sun as it appeared from behind the eastern wing of the courtyard. A guiding mark on the symmetrical axis would then be enough to provide an 'aim' for accurate sighting.

We can therefore assume that the slight declivity (approximately 5° if the elevations of the plans are correct) of the two buildings in relation to the east-west line indicates a ritualistic function. If this is so, the axis of the monuments (allowing for the height of the horizon seen from Monte Alban) would have marked sunrise at the equinoxes. This theory is based only on plans, and will have to be verified by observation on the site at the correct times. If it is proved correct, however, the orientation of the buildings would be relatively unusual, since the 17° declivity of Teotihuacan is more often encountered, and characterizes both the Chichimec city of Tenayuca and the Toltec city of Chichen Itza.

The site is characterized by another unusual building, in addition to the three monuments which vary from the dominant north-south axis. This is the Observatory (building J) which, with its strange arrowhead or wedge-shaped plan, is completely unlike any other construction in Monte Alban. Its longitudinal axis forms a 35° angle in relation to the rest of the ensemble. So far, there has been no scientific explanation of this plan, although it must have had some astronomical function, as was so often the case in the orientation of pre-Columbian buildings.

The presence of a 'tunnel' running through the building makes this a tempting theory; but the narrow arched passage is so oriented that an observer situated in its northern part and looking south cannot see the sky – he can only see the staircase on the south pyramid. And if he stands at the other end, facing north, his view is blocked by one of the projecting angles of the building. It is therefore unlikely that the passage was used to observe the stars.

The buildings at Monte Alban reveal architectural elements peculiar to the Zapotecs, and it is immediately apparent that a greater variety exists here than at Teotihuacan. There are eight principal forms: the pyramid, the temple combining pyramid and courtyard, the portico, the palace with patio, the ball-court, the observatory, and the tomb, sometimes surmounted by a funerary chapel.

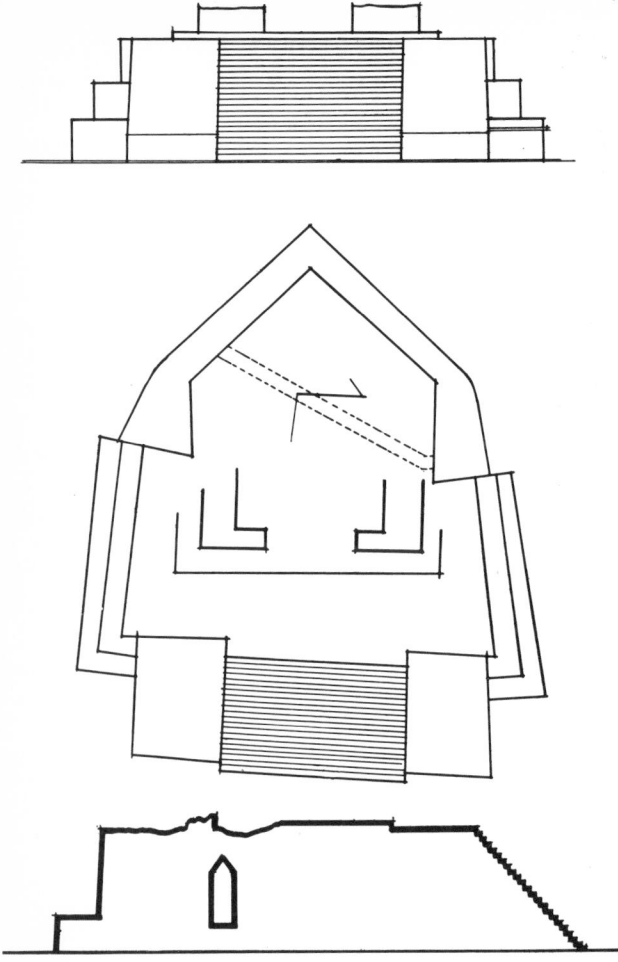

Elevation, plan and section of the Observatory at Monte Alban

The most important sacred building at Monte Alban is the huge square platform, 462 feet by 462 feet, that cuts off the south end of the esplanade. It is partially constructed on a natural eminence and has a staircase, 132 feet wide, leading to the upper level. This supports two small pyramids, one slightly behind the other, not for any axial reason, although their sides run parallel to those of the base. Both must have had staircases, one on its north and the other on its west face. Although it has not yet been fully excavated, the monument is approximately 82.5 feet high and dominates the sacred center.

North of the esplanade the horizon is blocked by a highly complex group of pyramids, platforms and courtyards. A staircase, about 231 feet wide and 33 feet high, leads to the summit of a building which at one time supported a magnificent portico, resting on some twelve thick masonry columns, 6.6 feet in diameter.

The columns are without doubt a Zapotec invention and date from Monte Alban II (shorly before the Christian era). They are one of the most important innovations of this civilization. They do not stand freely in space, but are always connected by some means to a wall, although they do not actually touch it. On the north platform, where they attain colossal proportions, their function is unusual: instead of merely shortening the lintels surmounting the entrance to a temple or palace, they combine here to form a kind of triumphal arch in three parts, giving access to a square courtyard situated some 9.9 feet lower and measuring 165 by 165 feet.

This construction is unique of its kind and is therefore worth special study. The Mayan triumphal arch, based on the false masonry vault suited to their concrete architecture, became one of the characteristic elements of their town-planning; but this formula was impracticable for a civilization that employed different methods of roofing. For this reason, the solution adopted at Monte Alban represents a primary achievement in the field of town-planning: it is both a separation and a connecting-link between two systems.

Due to the tri-partite arch, which provides an impression of 'transparency' similar to that of some Hellenistic stoas at Pergamum, and the alternating walls dressed on edge and flanked by columns which enlarge the bays, and because the passage is situated at the summit of a monumental staircase which leads to another staircase descending to an enclosed area of a completely different scale from that of the huge esplanade–due, in fact, to all these elements, the portico shows the effect of expert planning and achieves strong spatial elements.

To the north-east are a group of pyramids surrounding another smaller raised square. These buildings form a series of accents balancing the south platform and its two pyramids. At present, due to incomplete excavations, we cannot fully evaluate the arrangement of these groups–numerous features have not yet appeared. Nevertheless, the association of square courtyards and pyramids is clearly a spatial concept proper to pre-Columbian architects.

This characteristic becomes more complex in the great north courtyard; it is governed not only by the north-south axis, for a second pyramid, east of the ensemble, with a staircase on its west face, provides a second axis for the group. The dominant axis, however, is north-south, and its application is identical to that of the buildings M and IV. Once again, this is not accidental. The plan, as at Teotihuacan, relates a negative, concave space (the courtyard) with a volume in relief (the pyramid).

The effect is heightened in the north courtyard by the portico at the top of the staircase. Although there are no constructions at the summit of the staircases leading to the courtyards of buildings M and IV, the arrangement of space is nevertheless similar. It also resembles, to some extent, the Citadel at Teotihuacan, where the great axial staircase is not surmounted by a portico.

The similarity between these courtyards is all the more striking since they all, both at Teotihuacan and Monte Alban, have a small altar or shrine in the center, square in plan and sometimes provided with staircases.

The sacred buildings at Monte Alban include the group that extends across the central part of the esplanade forming, as it were, an intersection. There is a temple at either end, one facing north, the other south, each with a two-roomed sanctuary reached by a broad staircase. The area between them is bordered on the east side by a wide staircase leading to three separate sanctuaries, oriented to the east. The middle sanctuary is slightly higher than those on either side and is the most important; it consists of an entrance hall which leads to the 'holy of holies.' The neighboring sanctuaries had only one room, but they too had a pair of columns supporting a small projecting roof.

Here again we find the constants that also characterize Mayan and Teotihuacan temple-pyramids: the actual place of worship is usually very small (the general public was not allowed in the 'holy of holies' where sacrificial ceremonies took place), often consisting of two rooms, one built directly behind the other.

The priests' living quarters

While the plan of temples and sanctuaries is fairly straightforward, the same is not true of the interior arrangement of the palaces. Indeed, even the existence of palaces at Monte Alban has been strongly doubted, especially by Krickeberg, while Thompson did not accept the theory that the Mayans actually lived in their palaces. In my book on Mayan architecture I pointed out how only the demands of habitability could account for the complexity of some spatial arrangements. Since then, research at Teotihuacan and the restoration of the palace of Quetzalpapalotl have confirmed my theory. It seems wrong, therefore, to deny the Zapotecs what was clearly possessed by the Teotihuacans and Mayans. A simple study of the findings at Monte Alban shows that at least two of the great tumuli bordering the esplanade must have been the foundations of buildings which were the living-quarters of Zapotec dignitaries. This applies to building S and also to the more complex building known as 'Los Danzantes,' because of the stelae depicting dancing figures discovered on the base of the building.

Building S at Monte Alban is a square construction, about 66 feet by 66 feet, resting on a base scaled by a staircase slightly broader than the building above. An axial entrance leads indirectly to a central square patio surrounded by eight rooms, together with smaller rooms that must have been storerooms. This arrangement of rooms surrounding a kind of Roman impluvium closes resembles that of the palace of Quetzalpapalotl at Teotihuacan; we find the same proportions and the same general plan, except that there are no traces of a gallery or columns. The rooms are on a slightly higher level than the patio, and a few steps lead to them; this was to prevent flooding during the rainy season.

The 'Danzantes' group is constructed on a terrace, 198 feet long and 29.7 feet high, reached by a staircase 28.7 feet wide. In the center of the esplanade (66 feet by 148.5 feet) is a building similar to S, only smaller. The central patio, reached by an axial doorway leading into a vestibule, is surrounded by seven rooms, each measuring about 13.2 feet by 9.9 feet. Here, too, the patio is on a slightly lower level than the rooms. On either side of this square building (52.8 feet square) are two smaller constructions, bordering the north and south sides of the terrace. Built in strict symmetrical proportion to one another, they have two rooms each. A series of pillars forming a covered peristyle surrounds them on three sides – an original and practical solution for a hot country. This feature is the reverse of the interior galleries around the patio in the palace of Quetzalpapalotl at Teotihuacan.

It seems then that pre-Columbian living areas are not as simple in plan as was hitherto believed. The living quarters of the priests and dignitaries clearly formed part of the sanctuaries. There was therefore a civil architecture at Monte Alban as well as in other pre-Columbian sacred complexes. It is difficult to understand why so many specialists have been unable to accept a fact established merely by studying plans. The reason lies, perhaps, in the viewpoint of a particular archeological school of thought which always preferred only to see religious manifestations in the achievements of the past, and excluded all other theories; this reduces the fundamental motivation of man to a collection of beliefs detached from, and deprived of all practical reality. Fortunately, however, recent discoveries have shattered this myth and, as a result, our ancestors seem all the closer to us.

Roofing and decoration

With the exception of the interior passage in the Observatory and the subterranean tombs that we will consider, all the buildings at Monte Alban, as at Teotihuacan, had flat roofs, formed of intersecting beams embedded in stuccoed mortar. There is no evidence that this form of roofing was influenced by the famous Mayan vault; since whenever the latter was not used superstructures have disappeared, leaving only fragments of roofless walls. Fortunately, terracotta or stone models provide information about the roofs of both temples and palaces. We know that the profiles of cornices decorating the bases were identical to those on the summits. Furthermore, if we analyze the plastic vocabulary of Monte Alban, there are numerous analogies with Teotihuacan. The panel of Teotihuacan is replaced at Monte Alban by a motif with a similar function: it consists of a fillet surmounting the constructions. This projecting lintel is both strong and original in form, and to some extent resembles an architrave. It is accentuated by means of skewbacks placed at regular intervals, forming crenels in reverse; their alternating position creates a rhythm along the summit, and at the same time stresses the angles. These decorative motifs, survivals, perhaps, from an earlier wood architecture, may be the stone counterpart of projecting beam-ends. The shadows cast by the double projection of this molding accentuate the upper part of the walls and the plastic articulation of the architecture. Monte Alban employs sloping surfaces more frequently than Teotihuacan, but the profiles of cornices, which form 'steps' on the faces of the pyramids, also serve to interrupt the over-smooth forms of pyramidal plans caused by the direct tropical sun.

The volumes formed by abrupt projections and 45 degree slopes are expressed by simple but expert means. The profiles and vertical sections of the buildings are in this respect highly revealing. Research constantly indicates the same aim: that is to provide the outer surfaces of the pyramids with powerful volumes, despite the fact that architects could not exceed the natural slope because of the fragile masonry. The decorative formulae all stem from this requirement, and it governs all the methods used to construct series of steps and levels. Less systematic than Teotihuacan, with its ever-present panel, Monte Alban preferred to alternate inclined plans with vertical walls; although flexible, this formula does not lead to the strict, austere appearance of the City of the Gods. The width of the staircases at Monte Alban are perhaps its most striking feature – more so than those of Teotihuacan. They are a dominant and recurring theme in Zapotec architecture. Every building, whether temple or palace, is preceded by these great flights of stairs.

At Monte Alban, as at Teotihuacan, buildings were faced by a layer of polychromed stucco; the city must have been literally dazzling. This is why

the masonry today often seems neglected, its dressing neither even nor striking: all that can be seen is the enveloping layer of limestone.

The mystery of the 'Danzantes'

The unusual stelae discovered on the base of the palace of 'Los Danzantes' are the subject of much discussion. Carved in bas-relief, they are characterized by a sinuous continuous line, lightly hollowed out of large flagstones, sometimes 6.6 feet high. The motifs date from an early period and depict figures in unusual positions, suggesting some kind of dance – from which the name stems. The sculpture is undoubtedly influenced by Olmec art, and was probably executed in Monte Alban I, about 650 B.C., that is, before the end of the Olmec civilization. Monte Alban is located relatively near the lagoons of La Venta and Tres Zapotes, and the Olmecs were therefore the Zapotecs' closest neighbors. Some inscriptions found on stelae at Monte Alban are so like Olmec glyphics (the latter initiated pre-Columbian writing) that archeologists thought the earliest inhabitants of Monte Alban were Olmec tribes who had deserted their marshy regions.

This is a tempting theory, but it does not account for the often highly original character of Zapotec architecture. We must, therefore, continue to distinguish between the two ethnic entities, even if there are obvious signs of Olmec influence in the earliest forms of Monte Alban art and culture.

There are definite connections between the 'Danzantes' and some Olmec reliefs; yet the stylistic homogeneity of Monte Alban stelae indicates original inspiration, exceeding simple imitation. Theirs is a developed art, with definite and firmly established rules. Each figure – whether upright, crouching, crawling on all fours, or about to leap – is invariably presented with the head in profile. The faces and silhouettes are depicted with only a few lines, a striking feature. The figures are sometimes shown with beards, unusual for this clean-shaven

Reconstructed elevation of temple M at Monte Alban

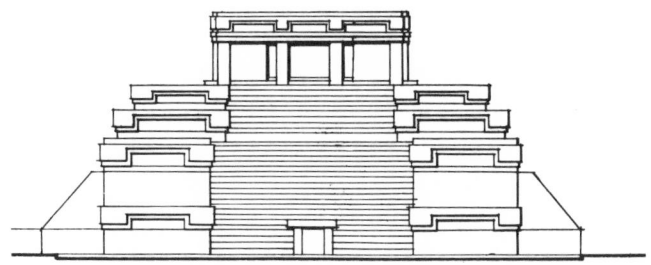

race. Many of them are wearing large circular earrings, similar to those frequently found in Zapotec tombs.

The stelae seem very primitive to us, consisting only of figures with curved 'elastic' contours – paradoxical when we remember the hard materials used in these megalithic works – but as the execution acquires strength, indicating both graphic and manual assurance, glyphs begin to be depicted with the human figures. At first, one or two signs are tentatively drawn near the mouth of a figure, perhaps expressing speech or even the name of the priest or god depicted. We are unable to decipher these glyphics (apart from the Olmec system of writing, this is one of the earliest testimonies of the pre-Columbian world), nor do we know much about the figures represented on the stelae. Are they kings, high priests, or divinities? The later stelae, similar in style to Teotihuacan frescoes, show a considerable increase in the number of glyphs, some having about twenty. They form a curving sequence of words coming from the figures' mouths. To some extent this foreshadows the 'funetti' or 'balloons' of contemporary strip cartoons.

One characteristic of Zapotec writing can never be sufficiently stressed: it is the relationship that exists between the numerals and those of the Olmecs and Mayans. This is particularly apparent in the system based on the period (representing unity) and the horizontal dash, or hyphen (representing the figure 5). Obviously this is a common tradition, since the similarities in such confined geographical limits are too striking to be merely coincidence. Furthermore, the analogies enable us to understand the relationships that also existed in the field of architecture.

The sacred games

The most outstanding influences of the civilizations situated south-east of Monte Alban are reflected in the sacred games played in the ballcourts. The founders of the game were the Olmecs, and they in turn bequeathed it to the Mayans. The Zapotec form of the game was clearly inspired by that of the Mayans, or at any rate by the same source as their writing.

We can trace a successive development of the form of the courts from those at La Venta, simply marked out by two parallel embankments, to the ultimate form found at Chichen Itza, Tula and, later, on Aztec sites. The Monte Alban form is a landmark in this evolution because of its relationship with, on the one hand, the Mayan game and, on the other, with the civilizations of the high plateaux.

The ballcourt at Monte Alban, as it appears today, consists of numerous superimpositions. Only the final version (enclosing three earlier structures) is sufficiently well-preserved to be of significance. It dates from the end of Monte Alban III, during the 5th and 6th centuries A.D.; we can therefore compare it with the second ballcourt at Copan which also dates from the 6th century (it too was covered by a third superimposition in the 8th century). Basically the courts are alike: they share the same proportions, the same shape, a flattened H, they both have horizontal, slightly sloped embankments, and there are no rings fastened to the summit of the embankments. The Monte Alban court, however, is a more advanced form, since its boundaries include walls enclosing both ends of the pitch; this was to become a standard form.

A feature of the Monte Alban court (135.3 feet long by 85.8 feet wide) is a kind of raised step with inclined planes situated at the foot of the horizontal embankments. This is found on almost all Zapotec monuments and, indeed, spread to other regions. At Manzanilla, north of Oaxaca in the State of Puebla, a ballcourt similar to that at Monte Alban has recently been discovered; and ruins at Yacundahui, near Mitla, excavated in 1960, reveal a form of ballcourt perfecting the plan initiated at Monte Alban.

Tombs and funerary sanctuaries

The Zapotecs always buried their dignitaries with great pomp and ceremony, surrounding them with precious objects. The tomb was usually constructed of broad stone slabs, similar to those of the 'Danzantes', arranged in caissons; at first the chamber was relatively small, but by Monte Alban II and III it measured about 130 square feet. The plan developed as the size of the chamber increased, and while early tombs were simple rectangles roofed with transversally placed stones resembling large monolithic lintels, the final forms were more complex: during Monte Alban II horizontally placed niches appeared, and gaining importance, soon resulted in a cruciform plan. As the chambers grew larger, horizontally placed flagstones were no longer adequate; in this way a purely Zapotec style of vault came into being – this can be seen in the corridor through the Observatory. A simple construction, it consists of placing two stone blocks at a steep angle, so that they touch and support one another at the top. Later, a third stone was added, trapezoidal in section, acting as a keystone between the two blocks. But this was not customary.

During Monte Alban IV (about 800 A.D.), the roofing of tombs resembles that of the classical Mayan period: it consists of a vault formed of three corbelled stones. The two horizontal blocks, projecting off the perpendicular above the horizontal wall, help to reduce the length of the third horizontally placed stone above.

The decoration of the tombs is also highly revealing. Some have polychrome frescoes that are obviously influenced by Teotihuacan pictorial art. The most beautiful is in tomb no. 104: its motifs bear a resemblance both to the later Monte Alban stelae, and to works in Teotihuacan. Although the borrowings from Teotihuacan III are obvious, there are also motifs which originated in Tajin, particularly the famous volutes characterizing classical Totonac sculpture; these, too, testify to the

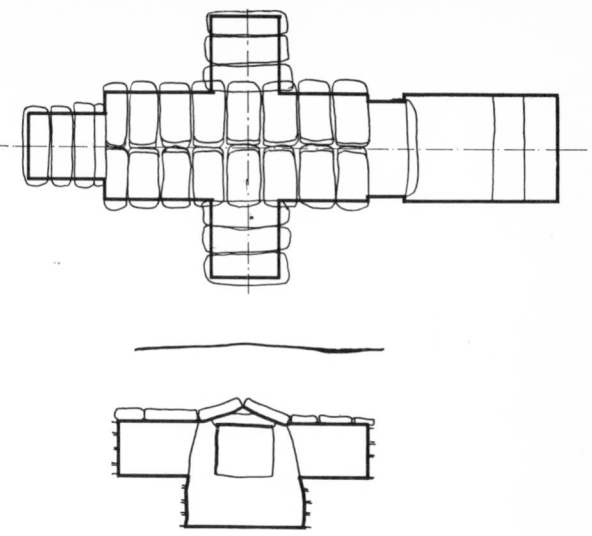

Plan and transversal section of a tomb at Monte Alban

close relationship of Monte Alban with the civilizations of the Gulf of Mexico.

The frescoes in the Monte Alban tombs show that polychromy must have played as important a role in Zapotec monuments as it did at Teotihuacan. At one time all Monte Alban buildings were probably faced with a thick, vividly-colored layer of limestone mortar. Today, the polychromy can only be seen in the tombs, although it was once one of the most marked characteristics of pre-Columbian architecture.

The tombs seem at times to have been only a subterranean part of a funerary sanctuary built above ground. The sanctuaries underwent an interesting development: they had a double chamber, as in the temples, and a vestibule with piedroits at the entrance flanked by circular masonry columns.

Very fine ceramic urns depicting Zapotec divinities were discovered on the lintels of the tombs. These are among our best sources of information on the pantheon of Monte Alban. As a rule, they surmounted the entrance to the sepulcher, as though providing the dead occupant with the protection of a specific god.

Yagul

Zapotec power now began to pass into the hands of a new people: the Mixtecs. A city characterized by this transitional period, and only recently excavated, is Yagul. Situated between Monte Alban and Mitla, and 9 miles from the latter, Yagul has an interesting plan, due to the development and expansion of palaces and living quarters reserved for the city dignitaries.

The architecture of Yagul marks an intermediary stage between that of Monte Alban and Mitla. The role of the sanctuaries is not as significant here as at Monte Alban, and it is the group of residential buildings set around square patios that is of primary importance. One part of the city has no less than six patios, arranged in groups 264 feet by 198 feet. Surrounding each patio are four long buildings with annexes, whose complex arrangement results in a kind of labyrinth. These ensembles have two types of plan and are constructed of rather rough materials, dressed with fragile mortar: in the first plan, the buildings are separated from the patio by galleries resting on columns forming a series of porticoes, at least three sides of which are in shade. In a less elaborate form this resembles the plan of the palace of Quetzalpapalotl at Teotihuacan. The second plan, however, lacks these galleries, and the buildings directly surround the patio. On the other hand, they have more than a single doorway: the façades have three entrances, separated by thick rectangular pillars.

The whole city is built in the form of tiers, also an interesting feature and Yagul was at its height during the middle of the transitional period, which started in Monte Alban IV. That the city had, however, existed from a much earlier period is revealed by remains dating from Monte Alban I. A number of fine tombs were discovered, but their contents are not as splendid as those recently found at Zaachila, another 'transitional' city; here remarkable Mixtec jeweled ornaments were discovered in a funerary chamber decorated with unusual reliefs executed in mosaic embedded in mortar.

The white palaces of Mitla

The mosaic reliefs lead us on to consider the splendid palaces at Mitla. Their renown rests basically on their ornamentation, although the distribution of space is original and reveals great plastic strength.

While Yagul was a city built on the heights in the sense that it was located near the foot of a rocky outcrop rising steeply from the center of a plain, with the summit crowned by a sanctuary, Mitla, on the other hand, marks a break with Zapotec tradition. No longer is the city built on a hill: it is situated in a relatively flat region, at the junction of a stream and the river Mitla, which waters the valley.

Mitla is one of the greatest manifestations of pre-Columbian architecture: the geometric motifs on the white façades of the palaces, reflecting the brilliant light, the huge rooms, the patios, the interior colonnades, the great quadrilaterals enclosing vast squares – all these constitute one of the major achievements in Central Mexican architecture. We are reminded here of the Quadrilateral of the Nunnery at Uxmal, in Yucatan, an example of Mayan genius both because of the planning and because of the treatment of the geometrically decorated façades. Indeed, Mayan influence is not inconceivable in Mitla: similarities between the Puuc capital, whose buildings date from the 9th and 10th centuries, and the Mixtec palaces are too obvious to be mere coincidences. At Uxmal, as at Mitla, the modernistic long horizontals and restrained decoration create a spectacular architectural ensemble.

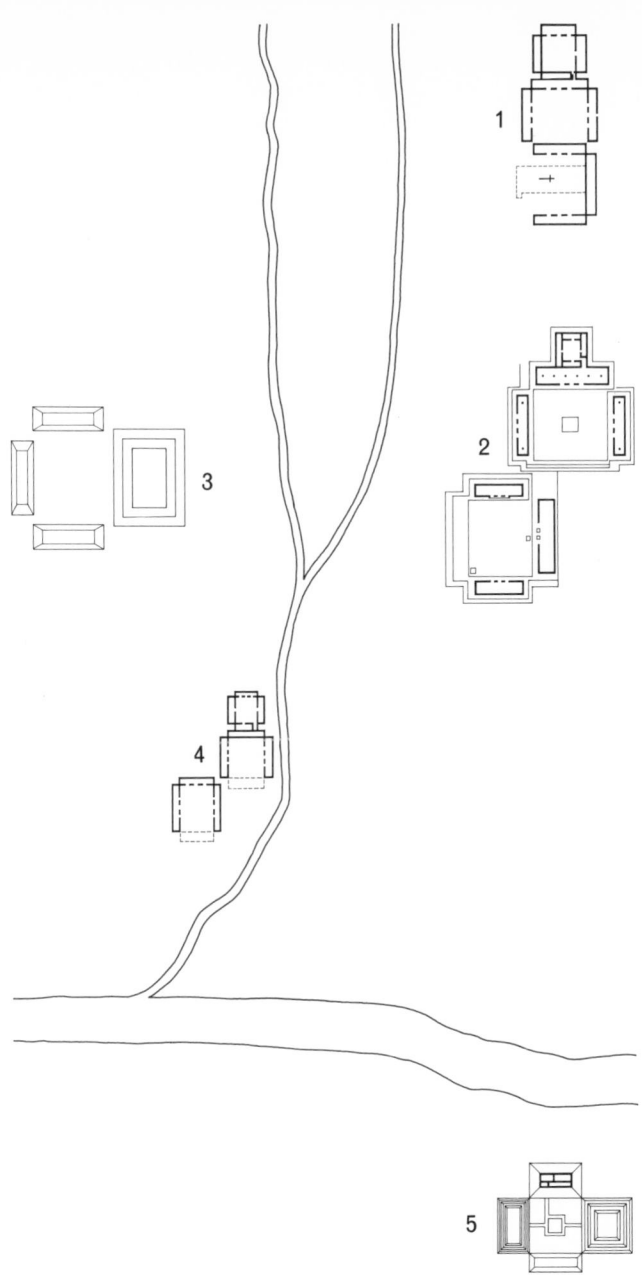

from 330 feet to 660 feet, the five groups of buildings at Mitla are oriented directly south. They consist of two types of structure. The center of two of the complexes (the 'Adobe' group and the South group) is formed by a rectangular or square space surrounded on three sides by palaces, the fourth and eastern side being blocked by a pyramid. These are probably the oldest groups and both are in ruins; only the bases of the palaces can be seen today. The rectangular pyramids probably consisted of three levels, but here, too, the superstructures have disappeared.

The other three groups are called the Group of the Stream, the Group of the Columns, and the Group of the Priest. The best preserved of the three is undoubtedly the Group of the Columns; and we will now examine its structure.

The Group of the Columns and the evolution of the quadrilateral

The two great courtyards of the Group of the Columns are not linked by one axis. The southernmost courtyard, which faces west, is surrounded on three sides by palaces 99 to 132 feet long. The patio is open at the corners, unlike the other two groups, where the palaces meet and cut off the corners. The arrangement, based on a quadrilateral with open corners, provided an unlimited view to the wings, yet at the same time allowed for what is virtually an enclosed space. It clearly avoided the impression of heaviness resulting from the juxtaposition of a central mass with two equally important wings. These quadrilaterals are very different from the patios of Teotihuacan and Monte Alban. Instead of the characteristic restricted, small impluvium, we now have a larger, more open central square.

At Yagul we can trace the development from the simple patio to the distinctive form of the quadrilateral. Here, buildings enclosing open spaces become progressively more independent until they are only connected at their interior angles; they are

Plan showing the position of palaces at Mitla. 1 Group of the Priest. 2 Group of the Columns. 3 Group of Adobes. 4 Group of the Stream. 5 South group separated, first on one side, and finally are freely articulated in space.

The quadrilateral may well be the result of a double evolution moving towards the same end: we know that the Mayans at Tikal already used a plan in which sanctuaries were built on all four sides of a square, with buildings facing in pairs, but with a marked vertical accent and the resulting angles being naturally open. On the other hand, Teotihuacan and Monte Alban palaces were arranged horizontally around an enclosed patio. The synthesis stems from these two forms. In one case palaces increased in size until they enclosed a square more than 132 feet wide; in the other, the role of sanctuaries was reduced (as an all-powerful, even hereditary priesthood developed) and replaced by living space for the priests and dignitaries. In this way sacred and functional buildings were merged. The architectonic evolution followed a definite pattern: while palaces that had developed from the simple dwellings surrounding the patio became detached from one another, pyramids became part of the dwellings which, by means of low buildings, increasingly enclosed the space. Mitla represents the meeting-point of these two streams: while the two earlier groups, characterized by the pyramid, are formed of separate elements, the palaces built around the patios grew larger, attaining a hitherto unknown size, and formed quadrilaterals which were at first completely enclosed, then open at the corners.

Geometrical mosaics

The central element of the Group of the Columns is the finest example of this palatine architecture: open to the south, the quadrilateral is flanked on its east and west sides by two palaces, symmetrical if only by reason of their tri-partite entrance which in both cases face west. The great palace that encloses the northern end of the square is the most interesting: on a high base is a terrace about 165 feet long, reached by a central straight staircase; the terrace

supports a building with beaten earth walls faced with stone mosaics.

The motifs of the mosaics are strictly geometrical and arranged in horizontal and skilfully articulated panels. Their variety – meanders, key patterns and lozenges – is extraordinary. Consisting of small blocks of thin tufa stone put together with admirable precision, the mosaics reflect the tropical light to perfection, particularly because of the slight relief of the walls. The refinement of the decoration is, in fact, closely related to the jeweled ornaments of the Mixtecs, masterpieces that represent the summit of pre-Columbian skill. The rooms surrounding the patio, reached through the great hall, are similarly decorated. Considering this magnificent decoration, Batres, who initiated restoration of the building, calculated that the Mixtecs had employed more than 100,000 finely carved stones for this palace alone. It was really sculpture. The earliest lintels at Mitla with similar ornamental treatment were carved into huge monoliths, sometimes over 20 feet long. Furthermore, the same technique has been found in motifs decorating cruciform-shaped tombs discovered beneath some of the palaces at Mitla.

Articulation of space

Access to the great hall of the palace at Mitla is gained by means of three doors located at the center of the south façade. The hall measures 132 feet by 24.75 feet, a surface area of about 3240 square feet – considerable compared to the tiny palace rooms of Teotihuacan (the hypostyle hall in the palace of Quetzalpapalotl totalled 1296 square feet while the actual living rooms never exceed 691.2 square feet) and Monte Alban (here rooms are never larger than 162 square feet). The central axis of this stateroom has six monolithic columns in a row, slightly conical in shape and over 12 feet high. At one time this colonnade provided the support for a timber and mortar roofing.

The north wall of this hall gives access to a narrow

corridor about 23.1 feet long; the doorway, however, is only about 4 feet high. After a sharp right-angled turn, the dark passage opens on to a small patio, about 33 feet by 29.7 feet, around which are four openings leading to living rooms. The largest room is on the west side and measures 56.1 feet long by 8.25 feet wide. The two rooms north and south of the patio are no larger than 33 feet long by about 10 feet wide. This ensemble projects from the northern side of the palace, whose plan thus forms a large, inverted T.

The facings of rooms and patio are decorated with magnificent mosaics, and must have been the private apartments of the rulers of Mitla.

Tajin: a magnificent jungle city

José Garcia Payon, who has been working on the site for the last thirty years, has still to publish his findings, but the actual plans of the city are revealing.

Tajin was one of the great capitals of ancient Mexico. Today it is part of the State of Veracruz and is located in the center of the hot lowlands of the Gulf of Mexico, north-east of Mexico city, and close to the oilfields of Poza Rica. The city consists of over a hundred mounds spread over a flat area, and an acropolis built on the hills bordering the plain.

Only some ten years ago the site was still overgrown with dense tropical jungle. What drew attention to the site was the Pyramid of the Niches or Alcoves, the only edifice not completely buried. The excavation of this unusual monument led to the discovery of the dazzling Totonac capital; and systematic disafforestation brought to light an extensive group of buildings.

Historical background of the Totonacs

The chronology of this tribe is valuable since it enables us to determine landmarks and, above all,

definite periods of evolution in this region; at the same time we can relate our findings to the already established periods of neighboring civilizations. This becomes an easier task since we have already pointed out the influences and connections existing between certain artistic forms of Tajin and, for example, Teotihuacan or Monte Alban.

Originally a clear connection existed between the art of the Olmecs (who occupied the coastal plain south of Tain) and the stone creations of the Totonac sculptors. Both used extremely hard material, similar types of ornamentation, methods of polishing, and both attempted to achieve homogeneous and completely self-contained forms. We must, consequently, assume that if the Olmecs left their mark on the Mayans to the south and the Zapotecs to the west, they must have had an even greater influence on the Totonacs to the north, who inhabited regions similar to their own.

The Totonacs who met Cortez when he disembarked in the New World, and with whom he allied himself against the Aztecs, were in fact the descendants of the Olmecs, a civilization that dated back to over a thousand years B.C. The early Totonacs lived and flourished at the same time as Teotihuacan II and III, and Monte Alban II and III, between the 1st century B.C. and the 6th century A.D.

Tajin fell into decline following violent upheavals (about which we know next to nothing), and after the annihilation of Teotihuacan, about the 7th century. Subsequently there began a second period of prosperity, influenced by northern newcomers, the Toltecs, and this was accompanied by a renewed interest in construction. Indeed, monuments on the acropolis at Tajin are clearly influenced by Tula. Towards the end of the 10th century A.D. the Toltecs were responsible for the renaissance of the Mayan city of Chichen Itza.

With the coming of the Aztecs, and the influence of Huaxteca, a third period followed. But by this time Tajin no longer existed; like the great classical Mayan cities it lay buried beneath tropical jungle. The Totonacs transferred their capital cities to Teayo and Cempoala, where the battle between Cortez and Narvaez was fought.

Plan of Tajin

The plan of Tajin, as drawn up by Payon, covers some 4 square miles; but this consists only of an area where extensive disafforestation has been carried out. Most of the sacred group of buildings is located between two small watercourses that join near the vast southern square, surrounded by four colossal tumuli, over 220 feet long and about 132 feet wide. A large ballcourt is situated next to this imposing group of pyramids. Consisting of two parallel mounds 198 feet long – similar to the La Venta ballcourt – its structure has still not been fully excavated. However – and this is an unusual feature at Tajin – it seems to have a wall cutting it off on the west side, while the lateral face of the south pyramid encloses it on the eastern side.

The number of ballcourts found at Tajin is exceptional: Payon has located six, and there may well be about ten more. As a rule the courts do not have boundaries at the extremities of the mounds, between which the game was played. The form therefore resembles that of La Venta; the relationship that existed between the Olmecs and the early Totonacs accounts for this.

S. K. Lothrop has put forward a tempting thesis regarding the use of certain Totonac stone objects, which resemble 'yokes' and ceremonial 'axes'. He suggests that these were employed by the participants in the game, as protection against the heavy rubber ball and to enable them to throw it over greater distances (we should bear in mind that players used their hips, and not their arms in this ballgame). The 'yokes' were worn around the waist.

North of the central square is another ballcourt, placed on a north-south axis. To the west, in the center of a complex group of buildings is a third ballcourt, whose vertical walls are situated along the base of the mounds, and whose extremities are ornamented with four magnificent bas-reliefs, dating from the Toltec period, but with volutes in the traditional Totonac style.

The center of this group consists of two platforms enclosing a fourth ballcourt; the northern platform is surmounted by two pyramids, classified as 2 and 5 in Payon's plan. The first faces east and the second north, and, due to recent restoration, both have regained their original appearance, with the exception of the upper sanctuaries which have completely disappeared – as is the case nearly everywhere in this region. Pyramids 2 and 5 are different in size but similar in structure; their profiles are characteristic of early Totonac architecture: a lofty base on an inclined plan leading to a vertical border interrupted by niches and surmounted by a broad projecting cornice. Two parallel staircases scale the first section of the pyramids, and a single broad axial stairway leads from the second section to what must have been the sanctuary on the summit.

The most characteristic feature of this architecture is the series of niches whose function resembles that of the 'tablero' at Teotihuacan, or the frames at Monte Alban. The deep recesses create dark areas further accentuated by the broad projecting cornice which, in turn, creates shadows stressing the different sections of the pyramid.

The pyramid of the Niches

These ornamental features are most prominent in the major construction at Tajin: the great pyramid of the Niches, numbered I on the plan. The pyramid rises from a square base (115.5 feet along one side) and consists of seven superimposed levels, a total height of 82.5 feet. Its eastern face is scaled by a broad staircase bordered on either side by a ramp decorated with key-pattern moldings in relief. Five structures project at regular intervals from the central staircase. Each consists of three small niches, surmounted by a broad cornice; they are constructed at the same level as the seven sections of the pyramids, and at even distances from one another.

The pyramid has a core of beaten earth, faced with stone; its faces all have the same decorative motif, consisting of square niches arranged around each section. The motif is highly original and indicates remarkable plastic strength; it is, furthermore, found on all buildings contemporary with the pyramid. Each level consists of a base with an approximate 45 degree slope. This supports a row of square niches whose recesses cut deeply into the structure. These in turn are surmounted by a bold projecting molding, almost as wide as the base. Each recess is set in a frame.

The niches are intriguing. Their function still remains a mystery: taking into account the niches that probably exist behind and beneath the great staircase, the total number is 365, corresponding to the number of days in the solar year. Again we have evidence that astronomical cosmology influenced the construction of pre-Columbian sanctuaries.

The uppermost storey supports a chamber; but it has not been possible to reconstruct this sanctuary.

The great staircase of the pyramid of the Niches ends on a square with, at its center, a square altar. On its east and south sides are two other pyramids. At the time of writing only the eastern pyramid (no. 3) has been restored and consists of five superimposed storeys. There are no niches. Each storey is slightly inclined and is decorated with broad panels with projecting frames. The staircase leading to the upper platform is located on the south face.

Tajin Chico, or 'lesser Tajin'

North of this complex rise successive 'landings,' obviously the result of extensive terracing. The group of buildings here are known as Tajin Chico (Little Tajin), and the esplanade leads to an acropolis surmounted by buildings dating from the Toltec period.

Before examining these monuments – they represent the final phase of the site's architectural evolution – we must first consider some of the highly original buildings on the lower levels. These are contemporary with the pyramid of the Niches. Unique of their kind, they show beyond doubt that Tajin produced the most inventive architecture of the pre-Columbian world.

Buildings A and C at Tajin Chico are perhaps the most striking and, at the same time, baffling of the group. Interpretation of these monuments is made more difficult because their forms are the result of numerous superimpositions and additions which probably altered the original concept. We are, however, concerned with the final stage which – despite damage caused by tropical vegetation – indicates that Totonac architecture has not yet been fully evaluated.

Building A apparently consists of a platform almost rectangular in shape, 115.5 feet by 72.6 feet and 17.1 feet high. The base is a small mound surmounted by a series of broad vertical panels crowned by a key-pattern frieze and a projecting cornice. Above are a series of chambers set around a central area from which they are separated by a corridor about 5 feet wide. The corridor (it was probably unroofed) is reached by an axial staircase located on the longest side of the building, and passing under a small corbeled arch. The solid mass that forms the core of the building and which is encircled by the corridor resembles the drum of a pyramid. It supports chambers (now in ruins) reached by a small narrow staircase on the south-west corner of the block. The function of the building has still not been fully determined. Eight chambers surround the central section (about 19.8 feet by 9.9 feet). Although badly lit, they were apparently used for living quarters, and can be compared to Mayan palace cells. Were the architects attempting here to perfect the Mayan method which ensured the rooms remaining cool and well-ventilated? Taking into account the torrid climate of Veracruz this seems likely. However, the system of roofing in no way resembles the Mayan vault, since roofs here are flat, with a framework consisting of beams embedded in mortar. Caso suggests a roofing formed of 'tiles embedded in concrete,' of which only the roots are today apparent.

Building C is on two levels (the west section is higher than the east) and consists of three superimposed storeys scaled by staircases on the west and east sides. The first two platforms are decorated with niches containing key-pattern motifs in relief, and are surmounted by broad cornices. The upper part of the building has a kind of portico with four bays on its east side.

The period of Toltec influence

Buildings constructed during later periods at Tajin often covered earlier structures. Prominent among them is building Q, also known the building of the small columns because of its unusual structure. Located at the edge of the acropolis, is consists essentially of a peristyle of fifteen columns on its longest side, and four on its shorter side. The height of these circular columns has not been exactly determined because of widespread damage; they are spaced at intervals of about 3.3 feet. The building is 66 feet long and only 9.9 feet wide, and resembles the peristyle of early Hellenic temples – minus the cella. This type of construction is unique in the New World, and we still know nothing of its function. Probably it stems from the architecture of Tula, since columns have been found all over this city; their role became so important that they replaced nearly all other forms of support, and permitted the construction of huge and elaborate hypostyle halls. The Court of the Thousand Columns surrounding

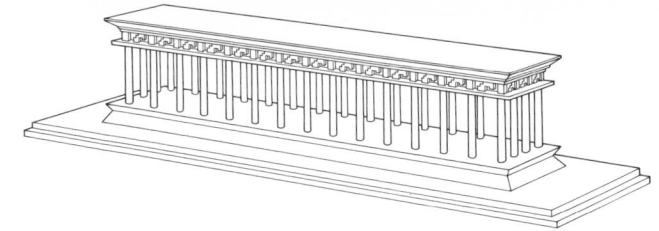

View of building Q, or the building of the small columns, at Tajin

the Temple of the Warriors at Chichen Itza is an example of this development. Building Q at Tajin Chico illustrates a similar evolution. Because of the impression of lightness, grace and subtlety it suggests, it probably represents – as far as we can judge from plans, sketches, etc. – one of the finest creations of pre-Columbian architecture.

The acropolis at Tajin dominates the whole site and forms a complex 429 feet long by 297 feet wide and 82.5 feet high. It consists of numerous superimpositions, some of which date from the time of the pyramid of the Niches. We are, however, primarily concerned with the final version. The summit of the three-storeyed pyramid supports a sanctuary whose east side is faced by a row of six circular columns, their stone drums measuring 33 feet in diameter. These are purely Toltec creations; indeed, the bas-reliefs that decorate the columns, set on either side of the entrance, so resemble those at Chichen Itza and Tula that it would be pointless to deny this. The highly original form of the hexastyle portico preceding the sanctuary is not unusual within the context of Toltec-influenced architecture; we have stressed the basic function of circular or square supports in Toltec plans.

Briefly then, Tajin clearly represents a culminating point in pre-Columbian architecture: only the appalling state of the majority of the buildings and the as yet incomplete work of restoration prevent us from according this site its rightful importance.

The sacred complex at Tlatelolco 1:2000

1 Platforms bordered with staircases
2 Small adjoining pyramids
3 The circular gladiators' platform
4 Two secondary pyramids with double staircases
5 The principal pyramid with remains of superimpositions
6 The pyramid of the Calendar
7 Church of Santiago Tlatelolco

Plates

Tenayuca (Mexico)

151 The double staircase of the pyramid of Tenayuca, ancient capital of the Chichimecs. Shown here is the next-to-last superimposition, of Aztec period, itself covered with a layer that was to preserve the building.

152 A 'Xiuhcoatl' serpent flanking a horizontal altar of the pyramid: this mythical animal, with its high crest, was one of the symbols of the god of the sun.

153 The final appearance of the pyramid, with its belt of serpents symbolizing sun and fire. These are rattlesnakes, as is shown by their tails in three parts, heavily scaled.

Santa Cecilia (Mexico)

154 Recently excavated and restored, this Aztec pyramid is the only one to still have its sanctuary and roof. Several superimpositions had preserved the building.

155 Following restoration work it is possible to gain some idea of the appearance of Aztec temples at the time of the Conquistadores.

156 The sanctuary containing the statue of the god. Before the entrance is a stone on which victims offered to the Sun were sacrificed by cardiectomy.

157 The decoration of the temple roof represents symbolically either stars or skulls. This pyramid was dedicated to Huitzilopochtli.

Calixtlahuaca (Mexico)

158 The circular pyramid of Calixtlahuaca, near Toluca. Dedicated to the god of wind, Ehécatl, one of the guises of Quetzalcoatl, the sanctuary consists of four superimpositions. The circular part dates from the third period, the last version being almost totally ruined.

159 The great staircase of the pyramid, dating from the fourth and final period. The sanctuary has disappeared.

160 The square pyramid on the upper esplanade at Calixtlahuaca. This building was dedicated to the god of rain, Tlaloc. In the foreground, a cruciform 'tzompantli.'

161 Detail of the 'tzompantli,' or skull-rack, with motifs in relief depicting sculpted skulls.

Malinalco (Mexico)

162 In a wild and impressive setting, Malinalco is perched on the mountain like an eyrie. Here the last sacrifices to Aztec divinities took place.

163 Cut out of the rock, the circular temple at Malinalco has recently been restored, together with the thatch and wood roofing.

164 The interior of the sanctuary: dedicated to the Aztec military orders of the Eagle and Jaguar, the building was cut out of the mountainside, a very unusual pre-Columbian method of construction.

165 Above, the jaguar at the back of the sanctuary. Below, one of the eagles placed on the circular ledge.

166 Aztec divinities protect the sacred place.

Tlatelolco (Federal District)

167 Excavated in 1963, in the heart of the Mexican capital, the site of Tlatelolco, of which only the remains of the great pyramid had hitherto come to light, formed part of Aztec Greater Tenochtitlan.

168 Details of bas-reliefs symbolizing the days in the Aztec calendar; they decorate one of the recently discovered pyramids. Above, the parrot symbolizing the fifth day. Below, the coyote representing the fourth day.

169 The pyramid of the Calendar: each of its faces has thirteen alcoves decorated with symbols of the days. The site of Tlatelolco, called today the Square of the Three Cultures, unites Aztec, Colonial and modern periods.

170 The sacred center at Tlatelolco, with pyramids, staircases and, at right, the gladiators' platform which is circular in plan.

◀ Plans

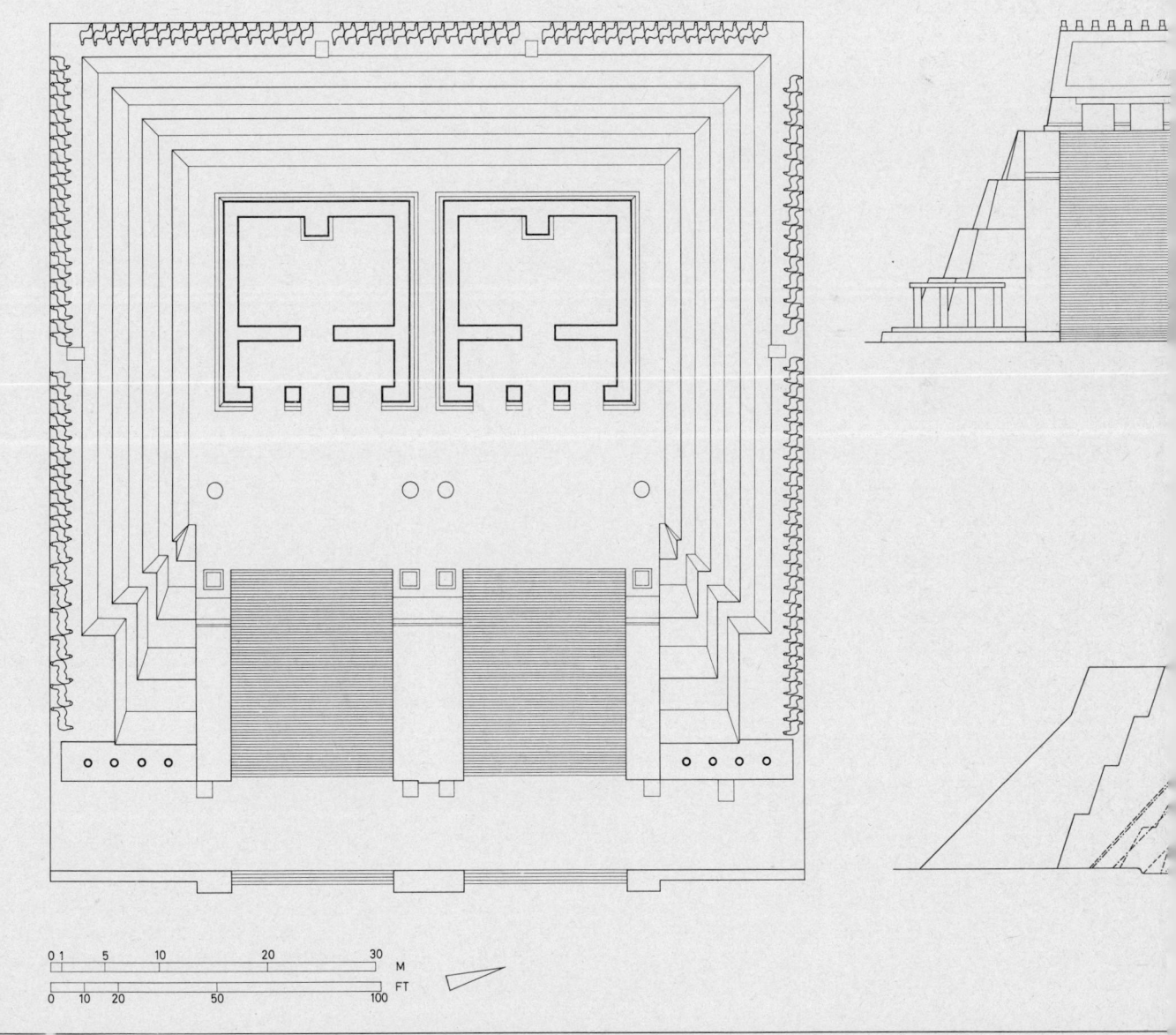

The pyramid at Tenayuca
Plan, elevation with restored sanctuaries and longitudinal section showing superimpositions 1:600

```
0 1    5    10        20           30   M
0   10  20        50           100  FT
```

Notes

Tenayuca and Santa Cecilia

Archeological work on these two neighboring monuments, both dating from the Chichimec period and both enlarged by the Aztecs, seems diametrically opposed. Two approaches are apparent: one – at Tenayuca – consists of preserving all the superimpositions that form a building, revealing them by means of tunnels, pits and cuttings. The other method – at Santa Cecilia – consists of revealing only the most spectacular stage of the construction, even if, in the course of finding it, this necessitates the destruction of numerous protective layers. However, the two approaches are not as different as they seem, for we must consider the state of individual monuments. Tenayuca has a succession of seven or eight constructional stages, both interesting and relatively well preserved; but Santa Cecilia's great pyramid was practically in ruins. For this reason, archeologists decided to restore only a small, almost intact, primitive sanctuary rather than show the superimpositions – which, in any case, were of indifferent aesthetic value. The two methods, carried out on neighboring sites thus complement one another, and provide information about the architectural cultures in ancient Mexico.

Tenochtitlan and the Aztec sites

Practically nothing remains of Tenochtitlan, the capital and largest city of the empire. This is due to two basic reasons: first, the cruelty and vandalism of the invaders who systematically destroyed palaces, living quarters and above all the detested sacred areas that had to be exorcised; second, the construction of a new capital on the same site. Consequently not only was every building torn down but all traces had to be removed before new monuments could be erected. The principal temples of Tenochtitlan in some respects influenced the establishment of the churches constructed by the Conquistadores. The religious symbolism had to be reversed: thenceforward Aztec divinities were considered devils, and the places soiled by the blood of human sacrifices had to be consecrated by sanctuaries whose purpose was to redeem the profanity of the 'idols.'

This explains why the Cathedral at Mexico is constructed on the foundations of the Tzompantli which stored the skulls of victims sacrificed on the summit of the great Teocalli. Similarly, the Spanish simply adopted Montezuma's seat of government. Here it seems that the actual arrangement as well as the dimensions of the present building are identical to those of the 'Casas Nuevas' of the Aztec emperor. Cortez wrote: 'In the city was Montezuma's palace, a building of such grandeur and beauty that I find it almost impossible to describe. I limit myself to declaring that its equal cannot be found in Spain.'

We can see why our knowledge of the architecture of the Aztec capital is slight; we have to be satisfied by sanctuaries in neighboring provinces, which give some idea of the splendor of the sacred complex at Tenichtitlan. Thus Calixtlahuaca provides information about the pyramid of Quetzalcoatl that faced the 'Templo Major,' besides being a good example of a circular pyramid. Thus Malinalco, with its entrance in the shape of the open jaws of the Plumed Serpent, gives an impression of the 'hell-house,' the 'horrific jaws' about to 'devour damned souls' – Bernal Diaz's description of the entrance to the temple of Quetzalcoatl. Santa Cecilia, too, has the appearance of any small pyramid on the outskirts of the great Aztec city.

Tlatelolco

Recent re-building in the heart of the Mexican capital supervized by Mario Pani included the tearing down of an ancient sector surrounding the Church of Santiago Tlatelolco and the College of Santa Cruz. The two buildings were known to have been erected over the ruins of a great pyramid which early historians rated as fine as the pyramid at Tenochtitlan.

Now, therefore, was the opportunity to verify the size and general plan of this sacred complex, which dates from the end of the Aztec period. (This will never be possible in the Zocalo area of Mexico City, since fine colonial buildings have replaced pre-Columbian remains.) The excavations have added much to our knowledge of Aztec town planning.

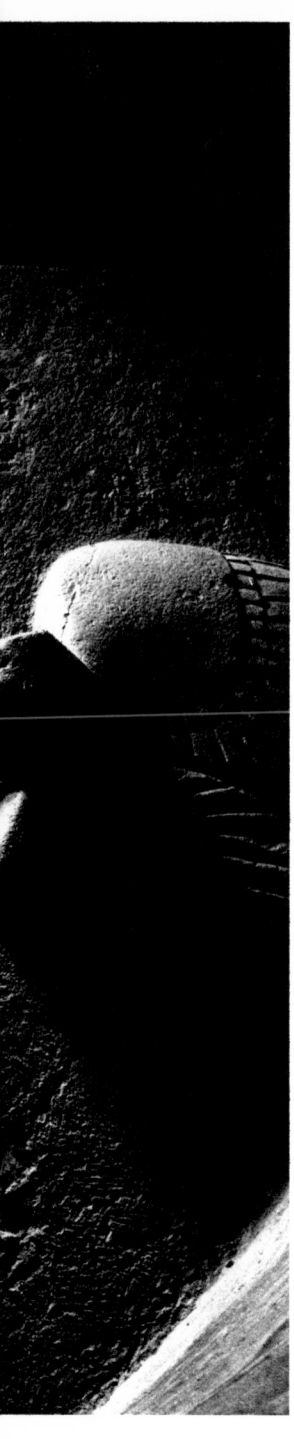

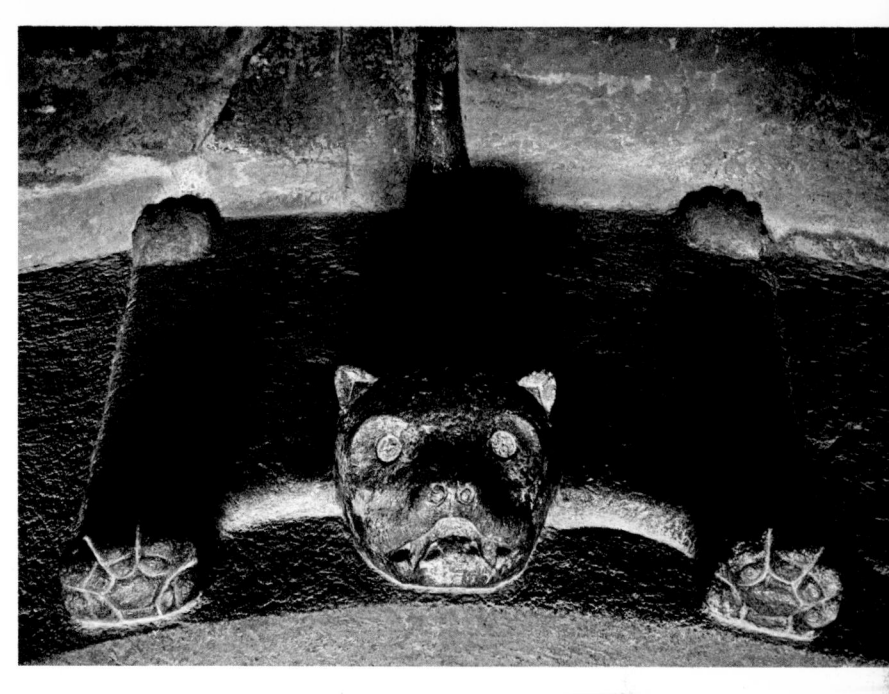

The sacred center at Malinalco
Elevation of circular temple of Eagles and Jaguars 1:400
Location of principal buildings 1:600

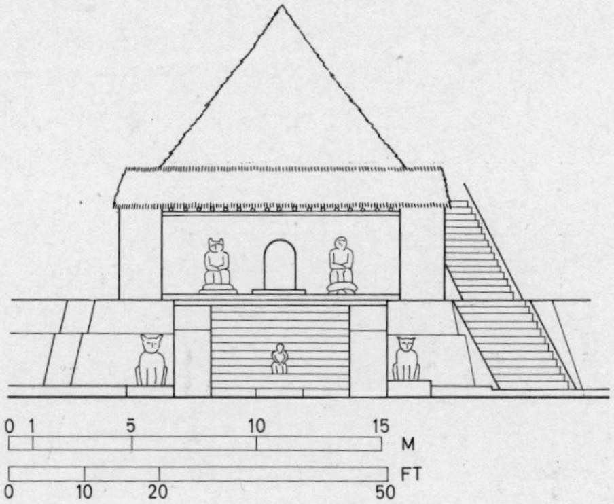

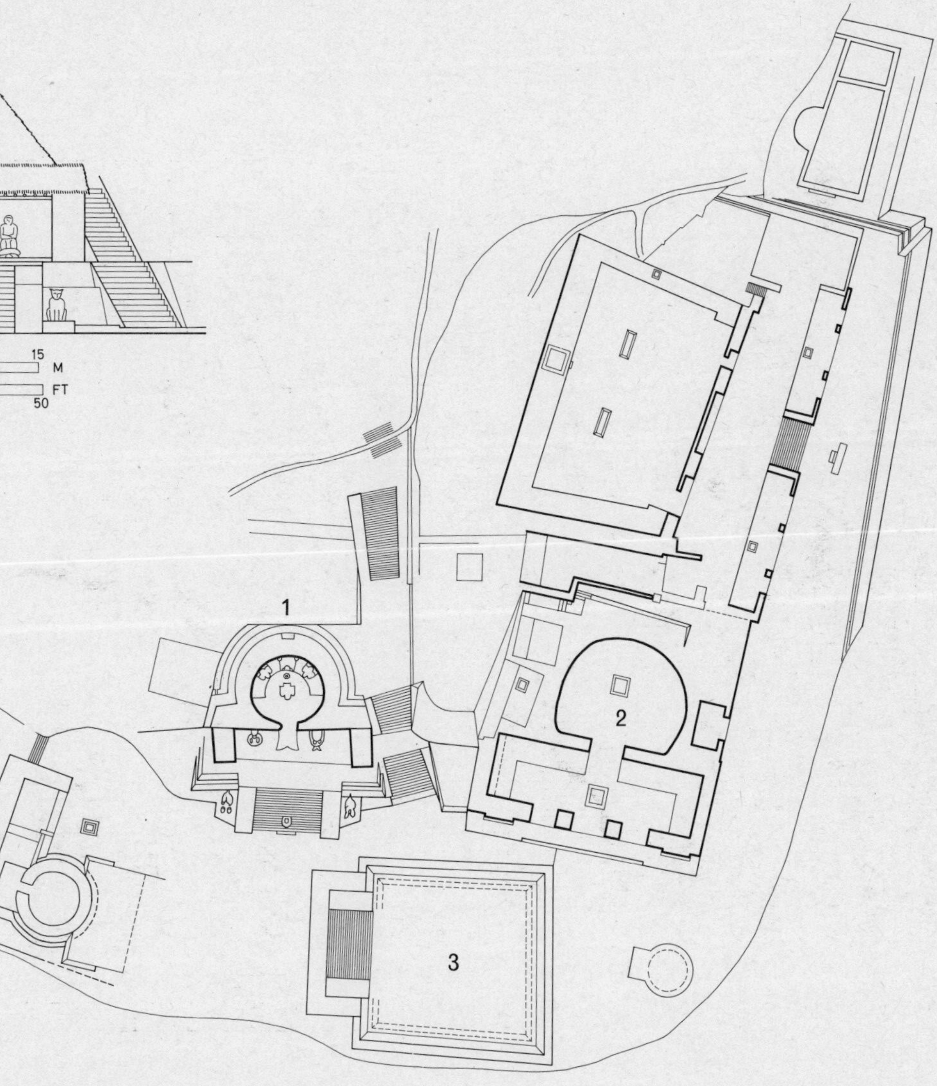

0 1   5   10   15
M
0   10   20   50
FT

1 The rock temple of Eagles and Jaguars
2 The second circular sanctuary
3 The square pyramid with two storeys

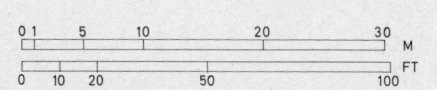

The circular pyramid at Calixtlahuaca
Plan of the final stage, section showing the four superimpositions, and elevation 1:300

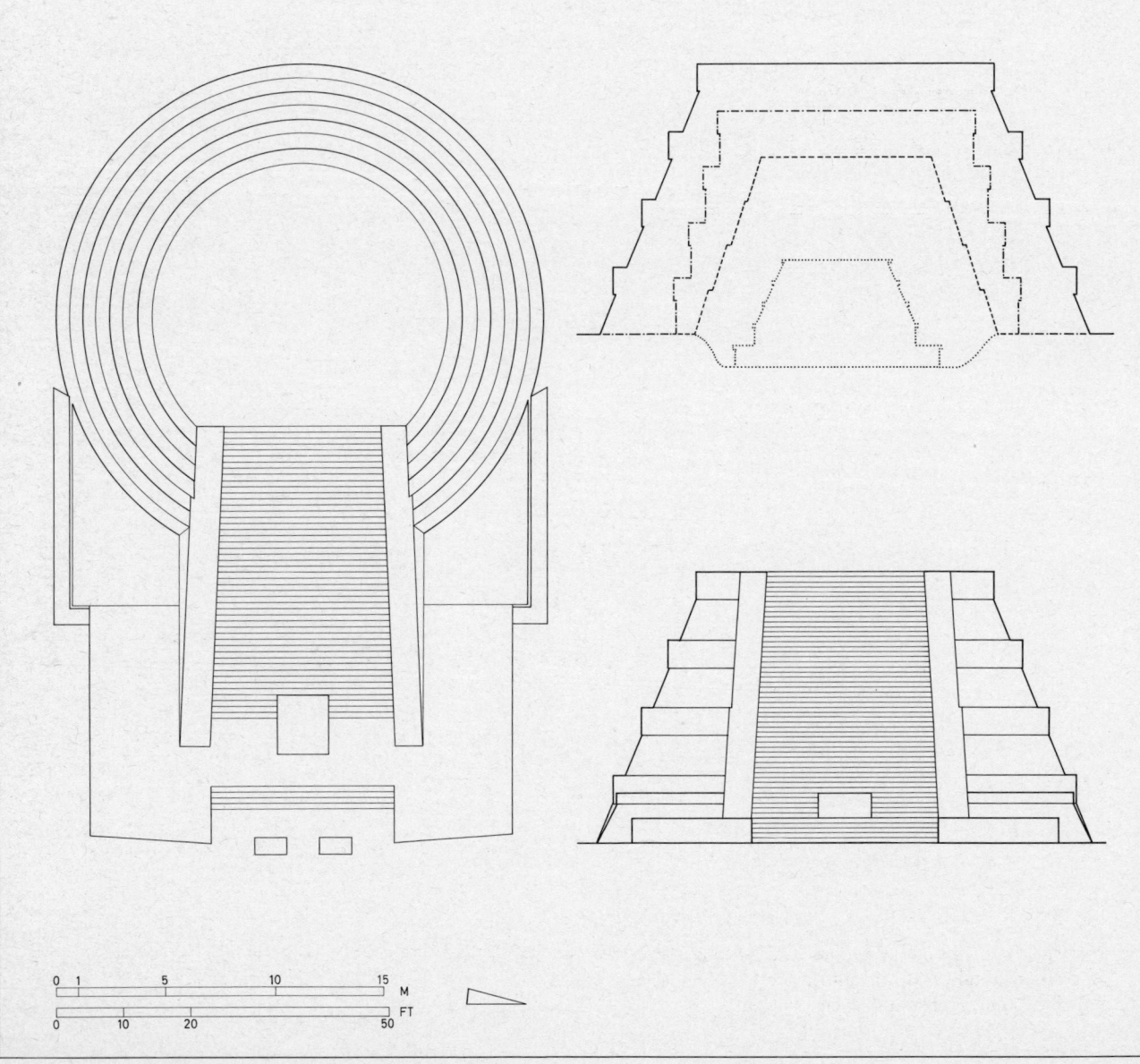

0 1 5 10 15 M

0 10 20 50 FT

5. From Toltec invention to Aztec synthesis

Returning to the high plateaux, which we left at the point when Teotihuacan had been twice invaded (the first, about 450 A.D. ruined the sacred center, the second, about 650 A.D. destroyed the whole city), we find the region in a state of unrest after the northern raids. Now the torch of civilization shone only in isolated areas, crossroads of influence that nonetheless were to provide the sources for the renaissance. The 7th and 8th centuries were Mexico's 'Middle Ages,' marking the end of the classical era. Subsequent civilizations had a new outlook and spirit, often very different from that of Teotihuacan, though continuity existed both in worship and in architectural forms. From what we know it is clear that a period of instability reigned throughout the high plateaux after the fall of Teotihuacan. Bands of semi-nomads systematically plundered settled communities. For this reason, any surviving small islands of culture consisted of strongly fortified cities on acropoli with natural defenses.

Xochicalco: a connecting link

The connecting link between old and new was in fact a city located outside the actual high plateaux. Xochicalco represents a new type of sacred center; situated at an altitude of some 5000 feet, on a 429 feet high acropolis dominating the plain near Cuernavaca (62 miles south of Mexico City), it is more closely related to the Zapotec cities than to Teotihuacan. Having withdrawn to their natural stronghold – which they further fortified in such a way as to create esplanades and terraces in addition to making the buildings impregnable – the citizens of Xochicalco now felt they were in a position to resist the disturbances of the 7th century.

Due to the highly accurate geometrical outlines of the retaining walls, which usually followed the natural contours of the hill, the plan of Xochicalco resembles some Mayan cities. However, the system based on two almost perpendicular axes – one running north-south and the other south-west to north-east – recalls some Hippodamian towns in Asia Minor, such as Priene, where the main streets scale and descend the steepest slopes of the acropolis rather than fulfil the demands of the base.

The principal avenue, built on a south-north axis and passing the pyramid adjoining the temple of Stelae, stresses the strict plan of the city, despite the natural steep ravines and twisted contours. There are signs everywhere of man correcting and modifying nature. Although the city spreads across several hills, linked by rectilinear avenues that solve the problem of different levels, it is dominated by a central area, measuring 3960 feet by 2310 feet. It consists of numerous pyramids, two ballcourts, living quarters and a subterranean vault, together with a principal pyramid-temple dedicated to Quetzalcoatl – its sides are decorated with magnificent bas-reliefs carved from large stone blocks.

The pyramid-temple was mentioned by early Spanish historians. Measuring only 69.3 feet by 61.4 feet, it is none the less distinguished by its outstanding artistry. It consists of two superimposed sections, the first 14.5 feet high, the second, now practically ruined, with a base only 5.3 feet high but which must originally have been 8.3 feet high. The monument is classical in structure, with a mound supporting a panel surmounted by a slightly projecting cornice. The actual sanctuary, whose interior must have measured about 33 feet by 33 feet, was probably roofed with joists supported by two pairs of columns, corresponding to the two pillars that subdivided the entrance into three separate openings; for, by projecting 24.8 feet, the bay would have been beyond pre-Columbian constructional techniques and ability.

Xochicalco is famous above all for the remarkable decorative sculptures on the faces of the pyramid-temple. The great plumed serpents, after which the pyramid is named, are arranged symmetrically in pairs on the sloping sides of the first storey, and form broad meanders which enclose small seated figures representing priests wearing sumptuous feathered headdresses. The serpents face inwards at the corners of the pyramid, with forked tongues protruding from open jaws. Hieroglyphics symbolizing fire and giving relevant dates, complete the ornamentation. According to archeologists the pyramid may well commemorate some major alteration in the pre-Columbian astronomical calendar, decided on during a priests' conference held at the time of the Feast of the New Fire.

A ballcourt, 231 feet long, was found in the lower section of the city. Its form is the traditional flattened H, and rings are fixed to each of the horizontally placed embankments. Constructed according to Mayan (Copan) and Zapotec (Monte Alban) plans, this court was to influence those built at Tula.

Recent excavations directed by Cesar Saenz have brought to light a very intersecting group of buildings, known as Group A, located near the pyramid of Quetzalcoatl. Particularly significant is the temple of Stelae, situated at the rear of a patio, flanked on either side by two symmetrical buildings, each containing an oblong room with an altar. The façade of this building forms the entrance to the patio, which consists of a double row of pillars forming a portico. It is reached by a broad monumental staircase.

The three stelae discovered by Saenz (from which stem the name of the temple) still puzzle archeologists, for they are clearly influenced by Copan; there are signs, too, of other cultures: glyphics from Monte Alban, and divinities which originated in Teotihuacan. When we also take into account the discovery of the 'yokes' at Veracruz, it becomes clear that Xochicalco represented a crossroads in pre-Columbian culture. It was a link, a survival from the past as well as a source for the future. It was to give the newcomers the seeds of a renaissance which first saw light in the city of Tula.

Tula: the evolution of interior space

While Xochicalco was flourishing, between the 7th and 9th centuries, the Toltecs, a warlike tribe who were responsible for the final destruction of Teotihuacan, were gradually becoming more civilized. During the 9th century they founded a great capital north of Teotihuacan: this was Tula, or Tollan. It was destined to revive the architectonic vocabulary of the pre-Columbians, and its influence was to be felt by both the Mayans at Chichen Itza and the Aztecs at Tenochtitlan.

The principal buildings of Tula are constructed around a square, 396 feet along one side. To the north is the temple of Tlahuizcalpantecuhtli, flanked by a series of hypostyle assembly halls (Toltec innovations), and to the east is the great pyramid, fronted by a large ballcourt whose mounds, some 215 feet long, have not yet been fully excavated; on the south side is a smaller mound which has still to be explored.

The most spectacular monument is without doubt the temple of Tlahuizcalpantecuhtli: a pyramid of five storeys, it is square in plan (125.4 feet along one side and 33 feet high) and is scaled by a 29.7 feet wide staircase constructed on the axis of the south face. The series of superimpositions covering the monument make it worthwhile attempting to find the original building. Additions to the east face covered a section of stone facing which is consequently perfectly preserved: it consists of an inclined structure surmounted by a panel and a broad frieze. The finely sculpted stone decoration reveals highly original motifs, among which are bird-serpents from whose jaws issue the head of a man, eagles devouring hearts, and passant jaguars with one front paw raised. These emblems represent the Toltec warrior 'regiments' of the Eagle and Jaguar.

The sanctuary on the summit has almost completely disappeared. Fortunately a series of monumental sculptures that supported the roof of the temple still exists. Enormous statues in relief, 14.9 feet high, resembling Atlases or Caryatids, in fact represent Toltec warriors with feathered headdresses, armed with broad breastplates in the shape of a butterfly. The four statues, together with four square pillars decorated with bas-reliefs also depicting warriors, must have been arranged in two rows in the sanctuary. The latter was some 66 feet wide by about 33 feet deep. In front of the entrance were two circular columns forming the body of a colossal serpent, its jaws open at ground level, and its tail supporting the lintel.

Although the temple is chiefly noted for its original and abundant use of ornamental sculpture, we must none the less emphasize the function of the supports, which made possible a sanctuary larger than had hitherto existed. However, its structure is in the tradition of, and represents an interesting development of the temple of Quetzalcoatl at Xochicalco. The principle of hypostyle halls marks the real architectural revolution, and the Toltecs were its first exponents. The buildings west and south of the temple are the most striking example of this.

With the arrival of the northern invaders, the whole socio-religious system seems to have been modified: and architects had to meet new requirements. The classical civilizations of Teotihuacan and Monte Alban had used vast quadrilaterals and open-air squares as meeting-places, but the Toltecs were to hold their assemblies in enclosed and roofed areas. Buildings were now constructed for the all-powerful ruling military oligarchy.

In fact, the structure of these halls had already been suggested by the enormous vestibule on the south side of the temple. A hypostyle gallery, with open façade, and an L-shaped plan that blocked the north-east corner of the great square, was constructed by means of three rows of pillars: 56 quadrangular supports enabled an area of some 960 square yards to be roofed. This is a remarkable achievement, especially when compared with the great entrance hall of the palace of Quetzalpapalotl at Teotihuacan, which covered an area of only 144 square yards.

West of the temple is a group of buildings, very original in conception, consisting of three assembly halls. Encircling each are a double row of square pillars and/or cylindrical masonry columns which form a broad covered area; light is provided by a small open patio. The largest of the three halls, 82.5 feet by 99 feet, has a total area of 900 square yards.

The flat roofing, formed of beams embedded in masonry (which, with the rest of the city was destroyed in the great fire), is supported by columns, ranging from twenty-eight to thirty-two in number. North and south of these three halls are galleries with porticoes supported by two rows of columns.

After the first Chichimec invasion (about the mid-10th century), the Toltec warriors apparently fled south; some settled at Tajin while the remainder continued until, 750 miles away, they founded a capital on the site of the Mayan city of Chichen Itza. The new city combined Mayan techniques – including their unique concrete vault – with those of the Toltecs, principally the hypostyle hall. However, a second Chichimec attack completed the destruction of Tula (1168), and Chichen Itza itself was destroyed during the 13th century, before the arrival of the Conquistadores. Nothing was left to posterity, yet the Toltecs' mastery of architecture was to be perpetuated by the Aztecs, whose reign also represents the culmination of post-classical cultures in ancient Mexico.

Aztec expansion

Unlike the Mayans, Zapotecs or Teotihuacans, the Aztecs created their empire by means of continual warfare. Their origins are a blend of fact and fiction. It seems that a tribe called 'Mexica' settled on a small island on Lake Texcoco. Underdeveloped and belligerent, they were thought to have come from the region of Aztlan (from which the name 'Aztec' derives). At first, the Aztecs were probably satisfied with their island, situated amid stretches of swampy water. They managed to eke out an existence under these difficult conditions, by fishing and cultivating crops on floating islands of aquatic vegetation. A courageous undertaking. However, the fertile lands of the central Meseta soon attracted them, but on arrival they found numerous communities – Toltecs, Chichimecs and, to the west, Tarascs – already established. Due to their agressive nature, the Aztecs – their capital Mexico-Tenochtitlan, in the heart of the plateau, was established in 1325 – were able in the relatively short time of a century to dominate the whole of the central region.

Their immediate ambitions fulfilled, the Aztecs looked farther afield, and their expansion was along truly imperialistic lines: they conquered the peoples of central Mexico – Mixtecs and Zapotecs – who were by now on the decline, then paved a way to the sea, subjugating the Huaxtecs and the Totonacs on the Gulf of Mexico; simultaneously they gained a hold on the Pacific coast. By the time the Spanish arrived in 1520 Aztec domination was absolute, and their empire covered an area larger than France. In the space of two centuries the whole of Middle America had come under the rule of a tribe which not long before had been barbarian. None the less there was constant rebellion among the subjected tribes and this was to help the Spanish cause considerably.

History helps us to understand the development of Aztec architecture in that it is founded on a combination of cultures, drawing on the most varied sources from which only the essentials were retained. The result, however, was in no way a hybrid, and creations stemming from innumerable pre-Columbian tendencies reveal remarkable unity. Aztec art is cohesive, even though some elements are clearly non-Aztec in origin. We know, for example, that Aztecs metalwork and jewelry were in fact executed by Mixtec artists.

A bloodthirsty religion

The Aztec buildings we propose to consider consist wholly of sanctuaries, for there are few traces of the great palaces of Tenochtitlan at which Cortez and his companions marveled. We must therefore attempt to evaluate Aztec religious beliefs before understanding the functions of the sacred buildings.

Aztec worship of divinities, together with the attendant culture, was based on varied beliefs, for the Aztecs were in the habit of including the gods of tribes they had subdued among their own. A similar phenomenon occurred in the Roman Empire: progressively influenced by their conquests, the Romans eventually erected temples for all their subjects in Rome. Fortunately we know much about the religious practices and cults of the Aztecs, due both to extant codices and to the firsthand, astute observations of Bernardino de Sahagun, a Franciscan monk who, a few years after the Conquest, recorded descriptions given to him by educated Aztec Indians.

Aztec temples, called 'Teocalli,' or houses of the gods, are generally built in twos – twin temples; they are dedicated simultaneously to two important divinities – for example, Quetzalcoatl and Tezcatlipoca, gods of Creation, the worship of Quetzalcoatl (the Plumed Serpent and the God of the Wind) can be traced back to the Huaxtecs and the Mixtecs, but especially to the great Teotihuacan civilization. Tezcatlipoca is represented by the jaguar, symbolizing darkness and night, and war. The form of worship also linked two other great divinities: Huizilopochtli, god of the Sun, and Tlaloc, god of Rain. Aztecs symbols frequently found include the eagle, jaguar and the coyote, representing warriors, as was the case in earlier Toltec cults. The eagle and jaguar symbolize human forces, whose duty was to supply the sun with the blood from hearts torn from living victims. With the Aztecs, the number of human sacrifices reached apalling proportions. Indeed, it was generally believed that law and order could only be maintained by the sacrifice of individual lives, whether in war or on the sacrificial altar. The universe had to be perpetuated, and since this was related to the sun, sacrifices were offered to Huizilopochtli.

At the dedication of the great pyramid of Tenochtitlan in 1487 more than 20,000 persons were sacrificed. These bloodthirsty orgies clearly required a regular supply of victims – hence the Aztecs' numerous campaigns, and their imperialistic attitudes.

The twin temples

Although the Aztecs inherited various pre-Columbian architectural elements their primary sources were close to the capital. A characteristic Aztec feature are the twin sanctuaries, foreign both to the Toltecs and Mayans, but interesting prototypes of which appear in the final periods of the Huaxtecs, the Totonacs at Cempoala, and the Chichimecs at Tenayuca. Never innovators, the Aztecs preferred to propagate a type of construction fulfilling their ritual and symbolic needs.

The pyramid is divided into two parts by parallel staircases, the upper platform supporting twin temples. This dual system stems from a concept peculiar to the cosmology of central Mexico, according to which the universe consisted of two inverted pyramids, their bases touching one another. The upper pyramid represents our world, and the lower – its summit located in the Antipodes – the next world. During the day, the sun scales one side of the first pyramid, reaching the summit at noon; it then descends along the other side. During the night, the process is reversed: the sun descends to the 'opposite' summit and rises towards the horizon (the base). It seems likely that the twin sanctuaries are an architectural attempt to reflect this duality. Clearly it was impossible to construct two pyramids with opposed bases; they are therefore juxtaposed. However, the double staircase and the two sanctuaries are clearly separated from one another.

Each storey of the pyramid – it consists of super-imposed levels, each receding from the one below – corresponded to a precise hour of the day, and also to a precise position of the sun as it moved through the sky. The cosmology as expressed by architecture is therefore logically consistent, and is apparent in a number of features of Aztec buildings.

The ornamentation of the sanctuaries is equally revealing: it always depicts the individual emblems and colors of the gods. The twin temples of Tenochtitlan, for example: the sanctuary on the left had a roofing decorated with vertical bands of blue and white representing the rain and the sky by day; the right temple roof was decorated with white circles set in relief against a black background, representing the stars in the night sky, and possibly also the souls of dead warriors. These white circles can be interpreted in a number of ways: in some cases, they are replaced by skulls – but these might well be stylized ears of corn. None of this is necessarily contradictory by pre-Columbian concepts; in fact the reciprocity of the symbolism adds to the representations. Roofs are furthermore surmounted by an ornamental border or frieze, whose crenellated motifs depict shells (the god of water, Tlaloc) and butterflies (the god of the sun).

Twin sanctuaries in the capital and its surroundings
Tenayuca

A study of specific buildings reveals the definite link between Aztec sanctuaries and those of their immediate predecessors, the Chichimecs. A case in point is the pyramid discovered at Tenayuca, in the suburbs of Mexico City, the capital in the 13th and 14th centuries of the invaders who destroyed Tula. The exterior of this monument has been systematically excavated, and is clearly Aztec in style; there are, however, a number of superimpositions, a constant in pre-Columbian architecture.

The pyramid at Tenayuca may well be the most outstanding example of superimpositions; there are no less than eight pyramids, each perfectly preserved within the next. The first version is tiny – only 3540 square feet – but successive superimpositions increase in size until the total surface area is some 5040 square yards, with a façade 214.5 feet high. The height of the top platform increases correspondingly from 26.4 feet to 62.7 feet.

The interest of superimpositions lies in what they tell us of the development of an art; above all we are provided with perfectly preserved constructions. The most unusual feature of the Tenayuca pyramid is the masonry border of sculpted serpents surrounding three sides of the building. They are carved in relief, in the shape of an S, with head of volcanic stone. The faces of the pyramid were punctuated by serpent heads and these projections animated the inclined planes. With its twin staircases, and twin sanctuaries (of which there is no trace today), the monument was undoubtedly dedicated to Tezcatlipoca and Quetzalcoatl; the latter was symbolized by the numerous serpent-like motifs surrounding the structure.

Tenochtitlan

We must take into account that most of the Aztec sanctuaries at the center of the capital were damaged or destroyed by the Conquistadores: the great pyramid of Tenochtitlan, located near Zocalo, almost on the site of the contemporary Cathedral of Mexico City, was completely destroyed. However, excavations in the basement have led to the discovery of parts of the pyramid's base, together with a few sculptures depicting heads of the Plumed Serpent. Archeologists have also established the exact position of the double staircase.

Tlatelolco

During recent construction at Tlatelolco-Nonoalco (where Mario Pani has just completed a model city for 70,000 people), workers came across a group of Aztec buildings. At one time bordering a lake, the area was formerly part of 'Greater' Tenochtitlan, which had some 500,000 inhabitants, according to the estimates of Jacques Soustelle – but not more than 100,000 according to Bernal. Naturally plans for the modern quarter were immediately modified to protect the Aztec remains. Excavations begun in 1963 around the pyramid, formed of fourteen super-impositions (which had been identified by Professor Pablo Martinez del Rio), enabled Professor Rul to bring to light a whole sacred center. On the face of a small adjoining sanctuary, he discovered a series of interesting reliefs depicting the symbols of the Aztec calendar. The huge sacred complex of Tlate-lolco included numerous other buildings: secondary pyramids, altars, 'tzompantli' or skull racks (plat-forms where skulls of victims sacrificed to the sun god were stored), gladiators' platforms, on which bound prisoners provided with ineffectual wooden weapons were forced to fight priests armed with sharpened lances and obsidian daggers, esplanades, broad staircases lining the principal avenues, etc. Today, however, the Tlatelolco group is a park, in the center of which is an early Baroque church.

Called the Square of the Three Cultures, the three principal civilizations that have formed and char-acterize Mexico today are represented here: pre-Columbian, Colonial, and Contemporary.

Teopanzolco

The condition of these Aztec remains – only a few years ago buried beneath a poor, overpopulated quarter – prevent a definitive evaluation of pre-Columbian constructional techniques. On the other hand, at Teopanzolco (State of Morelos), near Cuernavaca, there is a well-preserved double pyr-amid. The twin staircases and much of the super-structure forming the double sanctuaries are still visible. At the time of writing the temple is still being restored and will soon regain its original splendor. The monument is also of interest because

of the superimpositions which have come to light in the course of earlier investigations.

Santa Cecilia

Not far from Tanayuca, first a Chichimec then an Aztec city, is another pyramid, called the sanctuary of Santa Cecilia. Bernal Diaz del Castillo, an early Spanish historian, considered it even more re-markable than the sanctuary at Tenochtitlan – thus indicating its importance. After restoration by Pablo Martinez del Rio and Eduardo Pareyon, the pyramid, similar to that at Tenayuca, was seen to have a double monumental staircase beneath which were numerous superimpositions. One of the sub-structures was found not only to have retained its base but also a part of the upper sanctuary. For this reason the partially ruined layers were stripped away. As a result, the Santa Cecilia pyramid as it stands today is the only example of the numerous Aztec sanctuaries seen by the Spanish at the be-ginning of the 16th century.

Santa Cecilia has only one sanctuary; this is because the small pyramid that adjoined the build-ing dates from an earlier period, and its super-structure and sanctuary have disappeared. None the less the group provides valuable information on the original appearance of Aztec buildings. The almost modernistic appearance of the summit, with its framework of fillets enclosing white circles in relief, scattered over a dark background, the strength of the rhythms and volumes, even the surrounding landscape with its effectively placed branched cacti and aloes – all contribute to making this monument a jewel of Aztec architecture.

The circular pyramids

Another unusual type of construction was the cir-cular pyramid-temple. It consisted of a circular stepped pyramid, dedicated to Ehécatl, god of the air, and a relation of Quetzalcoatl, according to a Huaxtec concept. The monumental staircase that led to the summit of the conical shaft usually projected from the face. Circular pyramids are found in the Huaxtec and Totonac regions around the Gulf of Mexico, at Cempoala in Veracruz State, at Las Flores, near Tampico, at Huichapa in Hidalgo State, at Tamposoque, etc. Particularly noteworthy is the pyramid at Cuicuilco, the first stone construction of the central Meseta, located near the capital. During the Aztec period, the circular form was widely employed.

Calixtlahuaca

One of the best examples of circular Aztec pyramids is the pyramid at Caliztlahuaca, near Toluca, formed of four superimpositions. The great staircase dates from the final period; most of the circular construction is earlier, and is part of the third phase. It consists of four cylindrical concentric sections which are superimposed, and which supported a sanctuary, today no longer visible. The sanctuary was perhaps constructed of wood and beaten earth, and roofed with thatch, like most pre-Columbian temples.

Near this circular pyramid and part of the same group is a kind of small altar or platform in the shape of a cross, one of whose extremities is rounded. Motifs of skulls carved in relief project from the sides of this altar. This was, in fact, a 'tzompantli' or skull-rack.

Malinalco: an eagle's nest

The last Aztec creation was perhaps the most moving: it is a rock temple deep in the mountains at Malinalco, some 30 miles from Toluca. Malinalco is a very picturesque part of Mexico. Remote from civilization, reached only with difficulty, the temple was built during the final Aztec period, between 1476 and 1520; worship probably continued for some years after the Conquest. The reason we include this building among the circular temples is due to its interior, carved out of the rock mountain. Seen from the exterior, its staircases and squared storeys do not, in fact, suggest a circular temple. The numerous sculptures on the staircase are remarkable. The entrance to the temple is formed by the open jaws of a serpent, and leads to a dark circular hall. Along the back is a kind of raised ledge or 'bench' cut out of the rock and carved with eagles and a jaguar in relief. In the center is an eagle facing the entrance which he is clearly meant to protect. The temple is thus dedicated to the eagle and jaguar, which, as we know, played an important role in the worship of the sun.

The method used in constructing this temple in the mountain-side is unique, and accounts for the building being preserved. With the exception of the sculptures carved in high-relief and even in the round, the temple is intact. Moreover, the Instituto Nacional de Antropologia e Historia has replaced the thatch roofing of the temple.

We can now view the interior in its original light. The sense of mystery is poignant: nowhere else does Aztec architecture provide such a forceful impression; the visitor is enclosed in an area polarized by overwhelming strength. Mysticism is associated with exaltation. Malinalco represents the culmination of the worship of death and destruction, but it signifies, too, the unnatural silence that precedes war and bloodshed.

Town planning

Any survey of Aztec architecture must include the systematic town-planning that governed all buildings. Temples, often constructed on a huge square in the center of the city – the 'zocalo' of contemporary Mexican cities are the equivalent of these squares – were strictly orientated, and followed an orthogonal plan based on astronomical surveys. The observations of stars and planets on which the axes of construction depended, was also a ruling element of Aztec religion. The famous solar disc or calendar (now in the Museum at Mexico City), carved on a colossal granite block, provides notable proof of this system. The site of every sacred building was therefore fixed by the stars. Perhaps this also explains the superimpositions: under these circumstances, a new building could not possibly be constructed on another site. The only solution for changes or additions lay in covering the first construction with a new one, and the process was repeated. This feature also occurs in Europe: a baroque church often covers romanesque or carolingian structures which, in turn, conceal paleo-christian or even Roman foundations.

Earlier we mentioned that there is almost no trace left of civil constructions, such as palaces, baths, aqueducts, shops and markets. These must have been of considerable interest, judging by the accounts of early Spanish historians.

The admiration expressed by del Castillo suggests that Mexico-Tenochtitlan must have been a truly magnificent city. He writes: 'the palaces all shone brilliantly, their exteriors whitened with limestone, and decorated with greenery. We entered a vast courtyard first, then a hall with splendid furnishings. When we reached the great quadrilateral of the Temple, the square stretching before our eyes was larger than that at Salamanca; from the summit of the Temple, reached by 125 steps, we saw the towers of other temples sparkling with extraordinary brilliance. All of the houses had terraces; and towers resembling fortifications were erected on the causeways leading to the houses. On our return to the great square, many of our company – who had campaigned in numerous countries of the world, Constantinople, Italy and Rome – declared that never had they beheld such a well-planned and greatly populated square.'

Tenochtitlan during the reign of Montezuma II

These firsthand accounts enable us to form some idea of the splendor of Tenochtitlan at the time of the Conquest. The Aztec capital – which was then at its height – seemed to be the Venice of the New World. It was isolated on an island on Lake Texcoco, but connected to the mainland by three great dykes (one of which was five miles long), which, according to the Conquistadores, were wide enough to accommodate ten horsemen riding abreast. A geometric network of canals divided the different areas of the city into small islands. When the Europeans arrived the capital had already expanded to the banks of the lake, and must have covered about 4 square miles. It consisted of four main sections, the great temple forming the central area. The fourfold partition – each corresponding to a basic color in the Aztec cosmology – also had a social significance.

In addition to this easily defended position, the city also possessed an efficient system of fortification. The dykes were interrupted at intervals to allow the flow of water in the lake, the breaks being surmounted by wooden bridges. Where two dykes intersected a guard tower was provided, denying access to any hostile persons.

The insular position required extensive installations for the provision of drinking water, since the lake water was brackish. Two aqueducts were constructed, each with two conduits, so that cleaning or repairs could be carried out without affecting the water supply. The largest of the aqueducts was 3 miles long.

The military organization of the Aztec and Roman cities bear a resemblance: regular division of the ground corresponded to the centuria established by land-surveys; there was a similar maintenance of water supplies by extensive constructions; and the same politico-religious and, above all, architectural syncretism, existed. There is, however, one basic difference between the urban concepts. Imperial Rome was built of stone and marble, while Aztec Tenochtitlan was primarily a 'green' city. Cortez emphasized the part played by parks and gardens in the city. Each building was constructed around a patio and an interior garden. Today we can obtain some idea of this arrangement of canals and parks from the lagoons of Xochimilco, near Mexico City, with its water-gardens.

The religious and administrative center

The heart of this pre-Columbian capital consisted of two principal groups of buildings: the sacred center, and the complex of palaces and administrative buildings. The sacred center is the best known because of the numerous descriptions and drawings made by Sahagun showing the general arrangement; in addition excavations around the Square of the Constitution in Mexico City have revealed remains that enabled Marquina to draw up a plan siting the chief buildings surrounding the temple of Tenochtitlan.

Bounded by a crenellated wall encircling the 'temenos' this sacred center extended over an area of about 480 square yards, and was built along a north-south and east-west axis. The group was strictly orthogonal in plan and the principal pyramids were symmetrically placed. The first construction, along the west-east axis, is the ballcourt which, according to Sahagun, was built longitudinally, although borings indicate that it was perpendicular, that is, facing north-south. Next – still on the symmetrical axis – comes a circular temple dedicated to the god of the wind, with a staircase scaling the east face, thus balancing the double staircase of the great temple dedicated to Huitzilopochtli and Tlaloc. The mass of the temple measured 330 feet by 264 feet, its upper platform was about 100 feet high; this means that the roofing would have been at least 132 feet high. Left and right of the large monuments were two other pyramids, and a number of smaller buildings were arranged, often symmetrically, within the enclosure: 'tzompantli,' gladiators' platforms, small pyramids and altars dedicated to secondary gods. There were also sacred assembly halls, monasteries and novices' colleges, the living quarters of temple attendants. Sahagun notes 78 buildings, which probably include administrative buildings and palaces directly adjoining the sacred center.

The priests' living quarters adjoined the pyramids, as they had done in the Citadel and the Plaza de la Luna at Teotihuacan. But the Emperor's personal quarters were located outside the 'temenos.' According to early Spanish observations it was an enormous square building, 660 feet by 660 feet, provided with interior courtyards or patios. It was built on two levels. The emperor occupied the upper storey and the ground floor was given over to various administrative departments: public treasury, courts of justice, arsenals, etc. The reception hall could easily accommodate 3000 people, and the flat roof was large enough to hold a tournament of thirty horsemen. Other accounts describe the building as having at least three patios and about a hundred steam-baths, which the Aztecs called 'temazcal'; the system was probably similar to that of the Mayans.

The staterooms were vast, with flat roofing supported by rows of columns or pillars, resembling the hypostyle halls at Tula or Chichen Itza. The assembly halls thus stemmed directly from Toltec architecture. There is, however, no evidence of the Mayan or Mayan-Toltec form of the concrete vault. Ceilings consisted of sunken panels formed by sculpted beams. Walls were decorated in rich colors and sometimes hung with tapestries or vividly colored cloths. Floors were usually carpeted with rush matting.

16th-century codices and sketches show palaces set around patios. Pre-Columbian houses generally followed a centripetal plan, as at Teotihuacan and Mitla: palaces surround squares or quadrilaterals, rather like the Roman houses that surrounded an atrium.

The Quinatzin plan showing an Aztec palace at Texcoco, together with findings at Chiconautla,

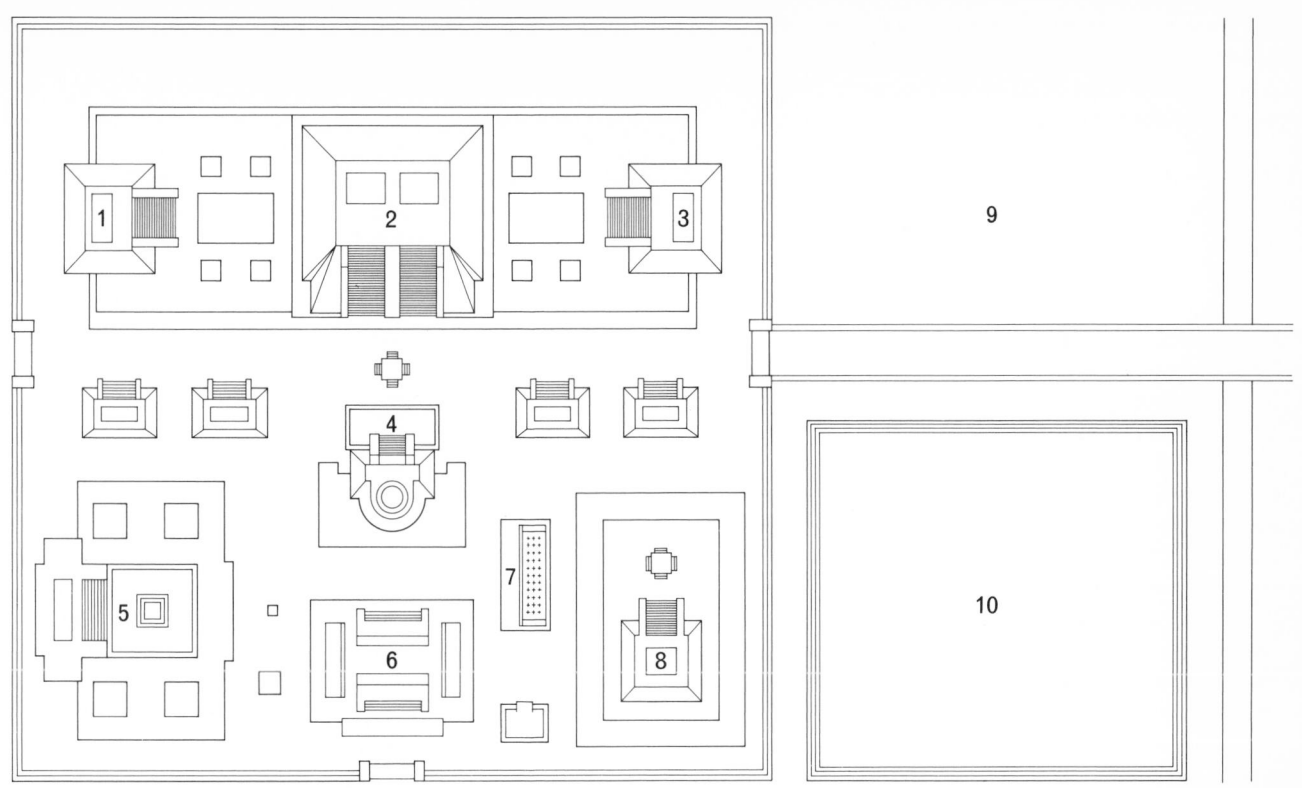

Plan of the sacred center of Tenochtitlan, as reconstructed by Marquina. 1 Unidentified temple. 2 Great pyramid, or 'Templo Major'. 3 Temple of Tezcatlipoca. 4 Circular temple of Quetzalcoatl. 5 Living quarters of priests and novices. 6 Ballcourt. 7 'Tzompantli', or skull-rack. 8 Temple of the Sun. 9 Site of the great palace of Montezuma. 10 Principal square

reveal similar constructions, where quadrangular patios are surrounded by halls or galleries with porticoes, behind which are the living quarters.

Destruction of a capital

Tenochtitlan was both original and pleasing to the eye, with its innumerable flat-roofed buildings, its walls of white lime, its gardens and canals, high pyramids surmounted by sanctuaries, long dykes and aqueducts. All the care and planning that constituted this great capital should have led to a renaissance of pre-Columbian architecture. Yet all was to be destroyed by the invading Conquistadores. The arrival of the Spaniards killed, in a short space, the promise of a dazzling society and culture. The art of Indian builders had developed so rapidly during the final five centuries that it undoubtedly would have resulted in outstanding masterpieces. The tragedy enacted at Tenochtitlan was the outcome of a total lack of understanding between two historically opposed cultures; the violence and barbarity of the conflict was such that it can only be described as genocide. The Indians of Mexico have survived, but their inheritance and culture have been destroyed; and of the splendor of Tenochtitlan only fragments remain.

Yet a tradition still exists. Today the seat of the Mexican Government is situated on the site of the 16th-century court of Montezuma II, and faces the Cathedral, erected over the great pyramid. It has taken Mexico five centuries to recover its individuality, to assimilate outside influences and to cauterize the wound inflicted by the European invaders.

If today Mexico has readopted the traditions of its early builders, if its rapidly developing architecture follows the pattern of its ancestors, this is largely due to the strength and vigor of the Mexican people. The different streams of pre-Columbian architecture were indeed converging towards an apotheosis that, because of the fatal encounter, never took place. Both at Chichen Itza, where the Mayan-Toltec renaissance died a natural death, and at Tajin, where evolution ended long before the Conquest, the final buildings indicate that a revolution was near. The Aztecs began to fulfil this: the Zapotec column combined with the Toltec use of interior space; town planning continued the legacy of the Teotihuacans.

For the first time, the construction of great assembly halls was sanctioned by a remarkable renewal of spatial vocabulary. Tenochtitlan provides the balance between religious and civil architecture. While Teotihuacan, Monte Alban and Tajin considered sacred buildings to be of supreme importance, Tula, Chichen Itza, Mital and, above all Tenochtitlan – the end of the pre-Columbian era – reveal a preponderance of buildings destined for civil use. Nowhere in Middle America did palaces reach the size of those in the Aztec period. Clearly distinct from sacred precincts, they had an autonomous existence which, with the exception of Mitla, was hitherto unknown. This autonomy is proof of the renaissance: it forced architects to consider palaces not merely as annexes to temples, but as individual entities. Consequently a centripetal architecture was no longer possible: the size and ornamentation of both palaces and their façades increased. Because of this, we can, at the end of pre-Columbian history, refer to an architectonic flowering based on the conquest of interior space.

In conclusion, we wonder whether this promise would have been halted yet again, as it was at Tula, Tajin, Chichen Itza and Mitla, or whether the development of the Aztec empire would have enabled pre-Columbians to progress beyond their limit (only exceeded by the remarkable creations of Colonial Baroque). What we know of Aztec town planning reveals that interior space increasingly corresponded to open space, patios and quadrilaterals. In this respect, the pre-Columbian world developed along the same lines as the great Western civilizations. This development, visible in the line linking Teotihuacan to Tenochtitlan, is based as much on technological knowledge as on social and religious requirements. Changes in cults were in part responsible for this development, since an increasing part of society participated in rites and an increasingly specialized administration was therefore needed.

More than a straightforward reproduction of the evolution of the West, the history of ancient Mexico provides us with something exceeding temporal contingencies: the dynamic town plan of Teotihuacan, the 'green' city of Tenochtitlan, the sense of geometric ornamentation at Mitla, the use of great open spaces whose impact is even more marked than that of enclosed spaces – all contributes a legacy for architecture everywhere.

Central Mexican Plateaux			Southern Mexico	
Xochicalco	Toltecs	Chichimecs and Aztecs	Zapotecs	Mix
600				
650 Xochicalco		650 Chichimecs I Nordic invaders overwhelm Teotihuacan	650 Monte Alban III B	69
700				
800			800 Monte Alban IV in decline	
	856 Foundation of Tula			
900				
End of Xochicalco Xochicalco IIII	967 Departure of Toltec expedition to Tajin and Chichen Itza			100
1000				
1100		1100 Chimecs II Foundation of Tenayuca		
	1168 Destruction of Tula by the Chichimecs			
1200		1200 Emergence of the Aztecs	1200 Monte Alban V Mixtec tombs at Monte Alban	
1300				135
		1370 Foundation of Tenochtitlan		
1400		1450 Aztec imperialism	1455 Conquest of Oaxaca by the	
1500			Aztecs	
		1520 Confrontation with Cortez		
		1525 Fall of Tlatelolco		
1600				

1519–1525 Spanish conquest and general collapse of pre-Columbian cultures of ancient Mexico

◀ Chronological table

...ecs	Gulf Coast Totonacs	Peten and Yucatan Mayas	Periods and influences	
				600
Emergence of the Mixtecs	650 Tajin in eclipse	650 Beginning of great revival in Yucatan	VII c. Period of uncertainty and population movement.	700
		800 End of Copan	Appearance of post-	800
		869 End of Tikal	classical civilizations	
		909 Last Mayan date		900
	980 Toltec influence and renaissance of Tajin	987 Toltec invasion at Chichen Itza	X c. Toltec influence on Tajin and Chichen Itza	
Mitla the capital		Mayan-Toltec renaissance		1000
		1007 League of Mayapan		
				1100
		1185 End of the Toltec domination of Yucatan		
				dom
	1200 Tajin abandoned Fresh Totonac culture at Teayo and Cempoala	Slow decline of the Mayan world	XII c. Pipils invade Guatemala	1200
				1300
Zaachila the capital				
	1460 Totonacs submit to Aztecs		XV c. Wave of Aztec imperialism throughout Central America	1400
				1500
	1519 Arrival of Cortez		XVI c. Conquest of Mexico by the Spaniards	
				1600

Bibliography

Monographs

Acosta, J.
El Palacio del Quetzalpapalotl. Mexico, Memorias del Instituto Nacional de Antropologia e Historia, 1964

Aveleyra Arroyo de Anda, L.
La Estela Teotihuacana de la Ventilla. Mexico, Museo Nacional de Antropologia, 1963

Bernal, I.
Arts anciens du Mexique. Paris, Le Temps, 1962

Bernal, I.
Teotihuacan. Mexico, Instituto Nacional de Antropologia e Historia, 1963

Disselhoff, H.
Les grandes civilisations de l'Amérique ancienne. Paris, Arthaud, 1963

Drucker, P., Heizer, R., Squier, R.
Excavations at La Venta. Washington, Smithsonian Institution Bureau of American Ethnology, 1959

Hartung, H.
Teotihuacan, dans «Deutsche Bauzeitung», September 1964

Kidder, A., Jennings, J., Shook, E.
Excavations at Kaminaljuyu. Washington, Carnegie Institution, 1946

Krickeberg, W.
Las Antiguas Culturas Mexicanas. Mexico, Fondo de Cultura Economica, 1961

Krickeberg, W., Trimborn, H., Muller, W., Zerries, O.
Les religions amérindiennes. Paris, Payot, 1962

Lothrop, S.
Les trésors de l'Amérique précolombienne. Genève, Skira, 1964

Marquina, I.
Arquitectura prehispanica. Mexico, Memorias del Instituto Nacional de Antropologia e Historia, 1964

Moreno, M.
La Organizacion Politica y Social de los Aztecas. Mexico, Instituto Nacional de Antropologia e Historia, 1962

Pina-Chan, R.
Mesoamerica. Mexico, Memorias IV, I.N.A.H., 1960

Saenz, C.
Xochicalco, Temporada 1960. Mexico, Instituto Nacional de Antropologia e Historia, 1962

Soustelle, J.
L'Art du Mexique ancien. Paris, Arthaud, 1966

Soustelle, J.
La Vie quotidienne des Aztèques à la veille de la Conquête espagnole. Paris, Club du Meilleur livre, 1959

Stierlin, H.
Maya. Fribourg, Office du Livre, 1963

Stirling, M.
Stone Monuments of Southern Mexico. Washington, Smithsonian Institution Bureau of American Ethnology, 1943

Vaillant, G.
La Civilizacion azteca. Mexico, Fondo de Cultura Economica, 1960

General Works

Anales de Antropologia. Mexico, Volumen II, 1965 (chapter by I. Bernal: Teotihuacan-Nuevas Fechas de Radiocarbono y su Posible Significado)

Congreso Internacional de Americanistas, Actas y Memorias. Mexico, 1964 (chapter by Roman Pina-Chan: Resultado de una Correlacion de Cuadros de Mesoamerica)

Desarollo cultural de los Mayas. Mexico, Universidad Nacional Autonoma, 1964 (chapter by Alberto Ruz Lhuill Lhuillier: Influencias Mexicanas sobre los Mayas)

Middle American Research Records. New Orleans, Tulane University, Volume II, 1961 (chapter by R. R. Wauchope: Implications of Radiocarbon Dates from Middle and South America, 1954)

Acknowledgements

The author extends his deep gratitude to Professor Ignacio Bernal, Director of the Museo Nacional de Antropologia of Mexico, and to Professor Horst Hartung of the University of Guadalajara (Jalisco), who have read the manuscript and provided invaluable advice and information about discoveries that are as yet unpublished.

Thanks are also extended to the Mexican authorities, particularly the Mexican Tourist Board, the Secretariat for Mexican Tourism, and the Instituto Nacional de Antropologia e Historia, for their help and kind support throughout the author's stay in Mexico.

Acknowledgement is made to 'Cia. Mexicana Aerofoto, S.A.' for the aerial photographs they kindly provided, reproduced on pages 21, 24 and 67.

The author wishes to stress the important facilities accorded by Sabena Belgian airline on the Brussels–Montreal–Mexico route, and by Mexicana de Aviacion airline on the Mexico–Oaxaca route. He offers his special thanks to the national company of Mexican petroleum, PEMEX, for the aircraft chartered from Mexico to Poza Rica, and the helicopter flight over Tajin.

List of plates

List of plans

Printed in Switzerland